THE RATZINGER REPORT

THE RATZINGER REPORT

An Exclusive Interview
on the State of the Church

JOSEPH CARDINAL RATZINGER
with VITTORIO MESSORI

Translated by Salvator Attanasio
and Graham Harrison

IGNATIUS PRESS   SAN FRANCISCO

Translated from the authorized
German manuscript.
Italian version published
under the title *Rapporto Sulla Fede,*
©1985, Edizioni Paoline, Milan, Italy

Cover by Marcia Ryan

With ecclesiastical approval
© 1985 Ignatius Press, San Francisco
All rights reserved
ISBN 0–89870–080–9 (PB)
ISBN 0–89870–085–x (HB)
Library of Congress catalogue number 85–081218
Printed in the United States of America

TABLE OF CONTENTS

CONTENTS

CONTENTS

CHAPTER ONE

AN UNUSUAL ENCOUNTER

Passion and reason

"An aggressive German of lordly air, an ascetic who carries the cross like a sword."

"An earthy Bavarian of friendly visage who lives unpretentiously in a modest dwelling in the vicinity of the Vatican."

"An iron-clad cardinal [*Panzer-Kardinal*] who has never laid aside the splendid robes and the golden pectoral cross of a prince of the Roman Church."

"He goes around in a short jacket and tie; he often drives through Rome behind the wheel of a small car. Anyone seeing him would never imagine he is one of the most important personages in the Vatican."

These quotations (authentic, of course), culled from newspaper articles which appeared all over the world, could be continued. These articles (some of which were published in the Milan monthly *Jesus* and translated into many languages) were commenting on statements extracted from an interview granted to us by Joseph Cardinal Ratzinger who, since January 1982, has been Prefect of the Sacred Congregation for the Doctrine of the Faith. As is well known, this is the Vatican authority which up to twenty years ago, and for four centuries prior thereto, was called the "Roman and Universal Inquisition", or the "Holy Office".

After reading such contradictory descriptions of Cardinal Ratzinger's physical appearance, some malicious persons might still harbor the suspicion that all the other comments probably also fall short of that ideal of "objective news-reporting" so often discussed at professional gatherings of journalists.

Having no wish to voice an opinion on this particular matter, we shall limit ourselves to the reminder that there is a positive side to everything.

Perhaps in our case these contradictory "transfigurations" undergone by the Prefect of the Faith, penned by some (certainly not all) of our colleagues, are a sign of the keen interest aroused by our interview with the responsible head of a Congregation whose reserve was legendary and whose supreme rule was secrecy.

The event, in fact, was really unusual. On the days during which Cardinal Ratzinger made himself available for our conversation, he granted the longest and the most complete of his extremely rare interviews. It should be considered that no other personage in the Church—apart from the Pope, of course—could answer our questions with greater authority. As is known, the Congregation for the Doctrine of the Faith is the instrument through which the Holy See promotes the deepening of faith and watches vigilantly over its purity. Accordingly it is the custodian proper of Catholic orthodoxy. Not by chance does it occupy first place on the official list of the Congregations of the Roman Curia. In fact, as Paul VI wrote when he accorded it precedence over all the others in the post-conciliar reform, it is "the Congregation which deals with questions of greatest importance".

Given the uniqueness of the extremely lengthy interview granted by the "Prefect of the Faith"—and after a perusal of the explicit contents—one can easily understand why, with some commentators, interest has been transformed into passion, into the need to take a stand: *for* or *against*—a stand which, according to the state of mind of the particular journalist, also leaves its mark, positively or negatively, on Cardinal Ratzinger's outward appearance.

Vacations, Cardinal-style

As for me, I knew Cardinal Ratzinger only through his writings. I had never met him personally. Our meeting took place on August 15, 1984, in that small but celebrated city Italians call Bressanone and Germans, Brixen. It is one of the most important historical sites, known to the former as the Alto Adige, to the latter as South Tyrol [*Südtirol*]. It is the site where prince bishops once resided, the backdrop of the struggles between popes and emperors, a land of a friendly and—just as it is today—hostile encounter between Latin and German culture. Hence an almost symbolic site, even though it was not deliberately chosen. Why, then, Bressanone-Brixen?

Some may fancy that the members of the College of Cardinals, the cardinals of the Holy Roman Church, perhaps still view themselves as princes who, come summer, abandon their splendid palaces in the *Urbs* and betake themselves to a charming vacation spot.

The reality is altogether different in the matter of His Eminence, Joseph Ratzinger, Cardinal Prefect. He spends the extremely limited time during which he can escape Rome's torrid August heat in the not much cooler valley of Brixen. He does not live there in a villa or in a hotel, but in a seminary that rents out some rooms at modest rates: a source of diocesan income for the maintenance of the theology students.

Old priests, attracted by this modest and inexpensive summer resort, meet in the corridors of the ancient Bavarian edifice. Groups of German and Austrian pilgrims meet here to enjoy a welcome pause in their journey south.

Cardinal Ratzinger lives here, he eats the simple meals prepared for him by the Tyrolese Sisters, he sits at table with the priests vacationing here. He is alone, without the German secretary he has in Rome. Occasionally he is in the company of acquaintances who come to visit him from nearby Bavaria.

A young colleague of his in Rome told us of the intense life of prayer with which he checks the danger of being transformed into a bureaucrat who mechanically signs decrees, who does not concern himself with the humanity of the persons involved. "Often", said the young man, "he assembles us in the chapel of the palace for meditation and common prayer. He is constantly aware of the need to let our daily, often thankless work in dealing with the 'pathology of faith' become firmly rooted in a lived Christianity."

Left/right; optimism/pessimism

He is a man, then, wholly rooted in a religious life. And it is only by viewing things from his standpoint that one will really understand the meaning of what he says. From that perspective, all those schematic formulations *conservative/ progressive, right/left* which stem from an altogether different sphere, namely, that of political ideologies, lose their meaning. Hence they are not transferable to the religious perspective which, to speak with Pascal, "is of another order which surpasses all the rest in depth and height".

It would also be misleading to apply another clumsy schema (*optimist/pessimist*): the more the believing person makes his very own the event that absolutely substantiates optimism—namely, Christ's Resurrection—all the more can he summon up the realism, the clarity and the courage to call problems by their real name so as to tackle them without closing his eyes or viewing them through rose-colored glasses.

At a conference held in 1966, the former theology professor Ratzinger came to the following conclusion with regard to the situation of the Church and her faith: "Perhaps you were expecting a more optimistic, a brighter and more joyful picture. Perhaps there was also some ground for such an expectation. But it seems to me important that what at the Council made us joyful and grateful must now also be perceived in its twofold historicity and thus make us understand the message that it contains. And it seems important to me to discern the dangerous new triumphalism, a tendency to which precisely the very critics of the old triumphalism often succumb. So long as the Church is in pilgrimage on the earth, she has no ground to boast of her own works. Such self-glorification could become more dangerous than the *Sedia gestatoria* and the tiara, which are more likely to elicit a smile than a feeling of pride."[1]

His special awareness that "the place of the Church on earth can only be near the cross" in no way leads him to resignation. On the contrary. He states: "The Council wanted to mark the transition from a protective to a missionary attitude. Many forget that for the Council the counter-concept to 'conservative' is not 'progressive' but 'missionary'." "The Christian", he reminds those who still suspect him of pessimism, "knows that history is already

[1] *Das Neue Volk Gottes* (Patmos), 150f.

saved, that therefore the outcome in the end will be positive. But we do not know through which circumstances and reverses we shall arrive at that great finale. We know that the 'powers of darkness' will not prevail over the Church, but we do not know under what conditions that will transpire."

At a certain point he spread out his arms and pointed to his only "prescription" in the face of an ecclesiastical situation in which he sees rays of hope but also perils: "More than ever before the Lord today has made us conscious of the fact that he alone can save his Church. The Church belongs to Christ and she depends on him to care for her. We are called upon to work with all our might, without anxiety and with the composure of one who knows that he is a useless servant even when he has done his full duty. Even in this reference to our littleness, I see one of the graces of this difficult time." "A time", he continues, "in which patience, that daily form of love, is called for. A love in which faith and hope are simultaneously present."

To tell the truth (precisely in regard to the aforementioned "objectivity"), in the days that we spent together, I noticed nothing to justify the image of a dogmatist, of a harsh Grand Inquisitor that some wanted to pin on him. At times I did see him looking disturbed, but he could also laugh heartily when relating an anecdote or commenting on a barbed reply. Another character trait, coupled with his sense of humor, also contradicts the cliche of "Inquisitor": the ability to listen, the readiness to let himself be interrupted by questions and the willingness to answer everything with the most extreme frankness, while allowing the tape recorder to run. A man, in short, very remote from the stereotyped image that gladly presents the "Curia Cardinal" as a question-dodger and as a diplomatic recreant. As a longstanding journalist, one who is used to every kind of interlocutor (including high Vatican prelates), I must confess that I was often amazed that I received a clear and direct answer to each one of my questions, even the most delicate.

The "too much" and the "too little"

We submit his responses to the reader's judgment (whatever conclusions he may draw) just as we wrote them down, taking great pains to be faithful to what we heard.

It must still be pointed out that the texts—the articles as well as this book—have been reviewed by the party concerned, that he has approved them by declaring that he recognizes himself in the texts (not only in the Italian original, but also in the translations, beginning with the German, which is normative for many others).

We address this to those who—in a knee-jerk, spirited reaction to the foregoing remarks—may still harbor the suspicion that there is *too much* of the interviewer in the interview. Cardinal Ratzinger's approval of the text makes it abundantly clear that here it is no longer a matter of "Cardinal Ratzinger according to a journalist's portrait", but of the "Ratzinger who, after being interviewed by a journalist, has acknowledged the veracity of the interpretation", just as, moreover, he also seems to have authoritatively confirmed the long summary published in *L'Osservatore Romano*.

Others, in contrast, have voiced the suspicion that the text contains *too little* of us: as if it were a question of a "guided" procedure, a move within who-knows-what complex strategy in which the journalist serves merely as a straw man. Hence it will be fitting and proper to present the course of our conversation exactly as it unfolded—in its simple truth.

A general request for an interview had been proposed by my publishers. It was suggested that the article, originally planned for a specialized periodical, could be turned into a book—in the event that the Cardinal could make himself available not only for several hours but over a span of several days. After a short while, Cardinal Ratzinger's secretariat replied to the communication and, at the same time, invited me to Brixen. Here the Prefect, without any prior agreement, placed himself at my disposal with one condition: that he be allowed to look over the text before publication. Thus there was no prior contact and no subsequent contact or intervention, but complete trust and freedom (in manifest loyalty) for the writer. Among those who have implied a *too little,* there are perhaps also those who have reproached us for not having been sufficiently "polemical", "critical", perhaps even "tough" in dealing with Joseph Ratzinger. But these objections come from those who follow a brand of journalism that strikes me as being among the worst imaginable, namely, that journalism in which the interlocutor serves merely as a pretext that makes it possible for the reporter to interview himself, to express himself, as it were, in that he sets his view of the matters under discussion in bold relief.

We, however, believe that our true task as "informers", so to speak, is precisely *to inform* readers in regard to the standpoint of the interviewee and to leave the judgment to the readers. Accordingly it is a matter of so stimulating the person being interviewed that he explains himself, of providing him the voice for what he has to say. Our procedure with the Prefect of the Congregation for the Doctrine of the Faith in no way differed from what we have followed with others whom we have had the occasion to interview.

But we do not conceal (we state this exactly in order to avoid hypocritical lecturing on impossible "neutralities") that we ourselves are involved in the adventure of the Church at this turning point in her history: nor do we conceal that we availed ourselves of the opportunity to understand what is transpiring in an ecclesiastical sphere which, even though we are laymen, personally affects us. Even when we posed the questions to the Cardinal in the name of the readers, they were consequently also *ours* and accorded with *our* wish to understand.

A theologian and a pastor

It is beyond doubt that when John Paul II appointed Joseph Ratzinger as head of the former Holy Office, he had made a "prestige" decision. In 1977 Paul VI called him to be Cardinal Archbishop of a diocese with a glorious past and a momentous present, the diocese of Munich. But the priest who was unexpectedly placed at the head of this episcopal see already belonged to the circle of the most famous Catholic scholars, occupying a unique place in every contemporary history of theology.

Born in 1927 in Marktl am Inn in the Bavarian diocese of Passau, Ratzinger was ordained priest in 1954 in Freising (diocese of Munich). Author of a dissertation on St. Augustine and later a lecturer in dogmatics in the most famous German universities (Münster, Tübingen, Regensburg), Ratzinger has also published scholarly works as well as essays that have enjoyed a wide circulation and become bestsellers in many countries. Critics vouch that his work not only attests competence in special areas but also calls special attention to comprehensive questions, to what Germans call *das Wesen*, essence, and precisely also to the essence of faith and to the possibility for it to come to terms with the modern world.

Typical of this effort is his *Introduction to Christianity*, something of a classic which is being constantly reprinted and which has formed a whole generation of clergy who were raised simultaneously by the wholly "Catholic" and the wholly "open" ways of thinking generated by the new climate of Vatican Council II. The young theologian Ratzinger participated in the Council as an expert of the German episcopate. Here he won the esteem and the solidarity of those who saw in this historic gathering a singular, unique opportunity to adapt ecclesiastical practice and ministry to the times.

Hence he is a balanced "progressive", if one wishes to apply the aforementioned misleading schema. At any rate, Ratzinger's reputation as an "open-minded" scholar was confirmed in 1964 when he was numbered among the founders of the international periodical *Concilium* around which gathered the so-called "progressive wing" of theology. It is published by an impressive group of scholars with its own administrative center, "the Concilium Institute", in Nijmegen, Holland. It has at its disposal more than five hundred international contributors who annually produce two thousand pages of text which are translated into all languages. Twenty years ago Joseph Ratzinger was among the founders and leaders of a publishing operation which was to become a rather critical interlocutor of the Congregation for the Doctrine of the Faith.

What significance does this have for the man who was to become Prefect of the former Holy Office? Was it a false step? A youthful transgression? And what happened in the interim? A turning point in his thought? a "change of attitude"?

I asked him this rather jokingly, but the reply was prompt and serious: "It is not I who have changed, but others. At our very first meetings I pointed out two prerequisites to my colleagues. The first one: our group must not lapse into any kind of sectarianism or arrogance, as if we were the new, the true Church, an alternative magisterium with a monopoly on the truth of Christianity. The second one: discussion has to be conducted without any individualistic flights forward, in confrontation with the reality of Vatican II with the true letter and the true spirit of the Council, not with an imaginary Vatican III. These prerequisites were increasingly less observed in the following period up to a turning point — which set in around 1973 — when someone began to assert that the texts of Vatican II were no longer the point of reference of Catholic theology. Indeed it was flatly stated that the Council still belonged to the traditional, clerical moment of the Church and that it was not possible to move forward very much with such documents. They must be surpassed. Hence the Council was only a starting point. But in those years I very soon disengaged myself from the directorate as well as from the contributors' staff. I have always tried to remain true to Vatican II, to this *today* of the Church, without any longing for a *yesterday* irretrievably gone with the wind and without any impatient thrust toward a *tomorrow* that is not ours."

Going from theoretical abstraction to concrete pastoral experience, he continued: "I have loved my work as teacher and researcher. I certainly never aspired to head the administration of the Munich archdiocese and subsequently that of the Congregation for the Doctrine of the Faith. It is a difficult task. Yet, inasmuch as I follow the reports which land on my desk every day, it has allowed me to grasp what concern for the universal Church means. From my so uncomfortable post (which at least allows me an overview of the general situation) I have understood that a certain 'contestation' of some theologians is stamped by the typical mentality of the opulent bourgeoisie of the West. The reality of the concrete Church, of the humble (simple) people of God, is something altogether different from that which is imagined in the 'laboratories' in which Utopia is distilled."

The shadow of the Holy Office

However one may judge him, it is certain that the "Gendarme of the Faith" in reality is not a man who can be easily labeled nor a functionary who knows only ecclesiastical authorities and apparatuses: he is a scholar with a concrete pastoral experience.

But even the Congregation to the chair of which he has been called is definitely no longer that Holy Office around which an ominous "black legend" has formed (as a consequence of actual historical guilt, but also under the influence of anti-clerical propaganda in Europe from the eighteenth century to our day). Today it is precisely secular historical research that recognizes how much the real Holy Office was more just, more moderate and more prudent than a certain myth (which obstinately endures in the current conception) would have it.

Specialists, moreover, recommend that a distinction be made between the "Spanish Inquisition" and the "Roman and Universal Inquisition". The latter was founded in 1542 by Pope Paul III, who perseveringly tried to convoke the Council which went down in history with the appellation "Tridentine". As a first measure of the Catholic Reform, taken in order to stem the heresy which from Germany and Switzerland was threatening to spread everywhere, Paul III appointed a special commission made up of six cardinals

who were empowered to intervene wherever such intervention was judged necessary. At first it was not even a permanent institution, and there was no official designation for it.
Only later was it called the *Holy Office*, or the *Congregation
of the Roman and Universal Inquisition*. It was never subject
to encroachments of secular power, and it adhered to precise and legally secured procedures (at least when viewed
against the juridical situation of that time and the roughness
that characterized altercations). In this respect, the Spanish
Inquisition was something quite different: it was in fact a
tribunal of the Spanish King, an instrument of State
absolutism which was created originally to try Jews and
Mohammedans suspected of a "feigned conversion" to a Catholicism which was also utilized by the Crown as a political instrument. Not infrequently it acted in opposition to
Rome, where the popes were not sparing in censures and
protests.

Be that as it may, all this—and it applies to the Roman
ex-Inquisition as well as to the ex-Holy Office—belongs to
the past, beginning with the very names. As we heard, it
was the first Congregation to be reformed by Paul VI
—through a *motu proprio* of December 7, 1965, the last day
of the Council. The reform confirmed its task to watch over
the faith, although it changed its procedural rules. But it has
also been assigned a positive role—to make suggestions, to
make proposals, to offer counsel.

To my question as to whether this change from the post
(albeit under Rome's watchful eye) of professor of theology
to that of supervisor of theological activity has occasioned
difficulties, he unhesitatingly replied: "I would never have
been ready to accept this ecclesiastical office if my job were
primarily and preponderantly of a supervisory character.
With the reform, it is true that decisions continue to devolve

upon our Congregation that may also entail disciplinary interventions. But essentially they are coupled with a positive
mandate, precisely 'to promote sound doctrine in order to
provide preachers of the Gospel with new energies'. We are
of course, now as before, called upon to be vigilant, 'to correct errors and to lead those who have gone astray back to
the right path', as the document itself states. But this protec-
tion of the faith must remain coupled with its promotion."

A misunderstood service?

Nevertheless and despite any reform, many of today's
Catholics are unable to understand the importance of the
service that this Congregation renders the Church. The
Church, after being put in the dock, for her part has the
right to set forth her arguments. They correspond, if we
have rightly understood, more or less to what is found in
documents and promulgations and to what has been proposed by theologians, who defend its function as being one
that is "more than ever fundamental". Thus the latter say:
"An indispensable point of departure for an understanding is
and remains a religious perspective, outside of which what
is service would appear as intolerance, and what is concern
would appear as dogmatism. Thus when one adopts a religious perspective, one understands that faith is the highest
and most precious good—simply because truth is the fundamental life-element for man. Therefore the concern to see
that the faith among us is not impaired must be viewed—at
least by believers—as higher than the concern for bodily
health. The Gospel admonishes us not to fear those who kill
the body but rather those who together with the body can
also kill the soul (cf. Mt 10:28). The same Gospel, taking

up the words from the Old Testament, also reminds us that man lives not 'by bread alone' but above all by the 'word of God' (Mt 4:4). But that word, which is as indispensable as nourishment, must be accepted in its original meaning and protected from distortions. Therefore it is due to the scepticism regarding man's capacity for truth and to the consequent loss of the true conception of Church as well as to the leveling of hope to earthly history alone (where only 'body', 'bread', and no longer 'soul' and the 'word of God', are reckoned in the first rank) that many view the mandate of a Congregation like the Congregation for the Doctrine of the Faith as irrevelant, if not anachronistic or harmful."

The defenders of the Congregation of which Joseph Ratzinger is the Prefect continue: "Added to this, some facile slogans are making the rounds, one of which asserts that all that really matters today is *orthopraxis*, hence 'right conduct', love of neighbor. On the other hand, concern for *orthodoxy*, that is, for 'right belief', according to the true meaning of Scripture, which is read within the living tradition of the Council, occupies a second rank, when it is not downright alienating. This is a facile slogan because it is superficial: do not also the contents of *orthopraxis*, the love of neighbor, radically change (always, but today above all) in keeping with the manner and way *orthodoxy* is understood? We shall cite an example from the present-day thematic of the Third World and Latin America: what is the right conduct through which the poor are to be helped in a really Christian and consequently also in an effective way? Does not the decision for a right *behavior* presuppose a right *thinking*, does it not thereby itself refer to the necessity of a search for an orthodoxy?"

We must pose such questions to ourselves. As we were discussing these important questions before we engaged in a genuine dialogue, Ratzinger himself told me: "In a world in which, at bottom, many believers are gripped by scepticism, the conviction of the Church that there is *one truth*, and that this one truth can as such be recognized, expressed and also clearly defined within certain bounds, appears scandalous. It is also experienced as offensive by many Catholics who have lost sight of the essence of the Church. The Church is, however, not only a human organization; she also has a deposit to defend that does not belong to her, the proclamation and transmission of which is guaranteed through a teaching office that brings it close to men of all times in a fitting manner."

He would return to this theme of the "Church", as he himself said immediately thereafter, because in his view this is where one of the roots of the present crisis lies.

"Heresy still exists"

Despite the positive role that devolves upon the Congregation—I remark—it nevertheless retains the authority to intervene where there is a suspicion that "heresies" are afoot and are threatening the purity of the faith. To our modern ears notions such as "heresy" and "heretic" sound so strange that they must be placed in quotation marks. When they are pronounced or written, one feels that one has been transported to times long past. "Your Eminence", I ask him, "are there really still 'heretics'? Are there really still 'heresies'?"

"Allow me to begin", he replied, "by referring to the answer to this question given by the new Code of Canon Law, promulgated in 1983, completely revised after a labor of twenty-four years and adapted to the conciliar renewal. In Canon 751 we read: 'Heresy is the obstinate post-baptismal denial of some truth which must be believed with divine and catholic faith, or it is likewise an obstinate doubt concerning the same'. As regards sanctions, Canon 1364 stipulates that the heretic as well as the apostate and schismatic incurs excommunication *latae sententiae*. This applies to all believers, but the measures are even graver when applied to a heretic who is at the same time a priest. Thus you can see that even for the post-conciliar Church (to use this term which I cannot accept and I shall explain why), heretics and heresies—characterized by the new Code as 'punishable offenses against religion and the unity of the Church'—exist, and ways have been provided to protect the community from them."

He continued: "The word of Holy Scripture is valid for the Church of all times, just as man's capacity for error ever remains. Hence the warning of Peter to protect oneself 'from false prophets . . . false teachers, who will insinuate their own disruptive views' (2:1) is still relevant and valid. Error is not a complement to truth. One should not forget that for the Church faith is a 'common good', a wealth that belongs to everybody, beginning with the poor who at least are protected from distortions. Consequently the Church sees in the defense of right belief also a social work for the benefit of all believers. From this viewpoint, in regard to error, it must not be forgotten that the right of the individual theologian must be protected but that the rights of the community must likewise be protected. Naturally everything must always be viewed in the light of the great admonition of the Gospel: 'Truth in love'. Therefore excommunication, which the heretic incurs even today, is to be understood as a corrective punishment, that is to say, as a punishment that does not punish him but rather aims much more to correct, to better him. He who sees and recognizes his error will at all times be again received with open arms into full communion with the Church, like an especially beloved son."

Nevertheless, I remark, all that seems almost too simple and clear for it to correspond to the reality of our time: it hardly fits preconceived categories.

"That's correct", he answers. "Concretely, matters are not as clear as they are defined in the new Code (and it cannot be otherwise). Today we do not encounter this aforementioned 'obstinate denial' and this 'obstinate doubt' openly. It is to be expected from the outset that they nevertheless exist in a multi-layered intellectual age like ours, only they do not wish to appear as such. Today one frequently opposes one's own theological hypotheses to the Magisterium by asserting that the teaching office does not express the faith of the Church but only 'the archaic Roman theology'. It is contended that it is not the Congregation but they, the 'heretics', who represent the 'authentic' meaning of the transmitted faith. Where a still stronger ecclesiastical bond exists, we encounter similar but essentially related phenomena: I wonder at the adroitness of theologians who manage to represent the exact opposite of what is written in clear documents of the Magisterium in order afterward to set forth this inversion with skilled dialectical devices as the 'true' meaning of the documents in question."

CHAPTER TWO

A COUNCIL TO BE REDISCOVERED

Two counterposed errors

In order to get to the heart of the matter we must, almost of necessity, begin with the extraordinary event of Vatican Council II, the twentieth anniversary of whose close will be celebrated in 1985. Twenty years which by far have brought about more changes in the Catholic Church than were wrought over the span of two centuries.

Today no one who is and wishes to remain Catholic nourishes any doubts—nor can he nourish them—that the great documents of Vatican Council II are important, rich, opportune and indispensable. Least of all, naturally, the Prefect of the Congregation for the Doctrine of the Faith. To remind him of this would not only be superfluous but ridiculous. Oddly enough, nevertheless, some commentators have obviously considered it necessary to advance doubts on this matter.

Yet, not only were the statements in which Cardinal Ratzinger defended Vatican II and its decisions eminently clear, but he repeatedly corroborated them at every opportunity.

Among countless examples, I shall cite an article he wrote in 1975 on the occasion of the tenth anniversary of the close of the Council. I reread the text of that article to him in Brixen, and he confirmed to me that he still wholly recognized himself therein.

Thus ten years before our conversation, he had already written: "Vatican II today stands in a twilight. For a long time it has been regarded by the so-called progressive wing as completely surpassed and, consequently, as a thing of the past, no longer relevant to the present. By the opposite side, the 'conservative' wing, it is, conversely, viewed as the cause of the present decadence of the Catholic Church and even judged as an apostasy from Vatican I and from the Council of Trent. Consequently demands have been made for its retraction or for a revision that would be tantamount to a retraction."[1]

Thereupon he continued: "Over against both tendencies, before all else, it must be stated that Vatican II is upheld by the same authority as Vatican I and the Council of Trent, namely, the Pope and the College of Bishops in communion with him, and that also with regard to its contents, Vatican II is in the strictest continuity with both previous councils and incorporates their texts word for word in decisive points."[2]

From this Ratzinger drew two conclusions. *First*: "It is impossible ('for a Catholic') to take a position *for* or *against* Trent or Vatican I. Whoever accepts Vatican II, as it has clearly expressed and understood itself, at the same time accepts the whole binding tradition of the Catholic Church, particularly also the two previous councils. And that also applies to the so-called 'progressivism', at least in its extreme forms." *Second*: "It is likewise impossible to decide *in favor* of Trent and Vatican I, but *against* Vatican II. Whoever denies Vatican II denies the authority that upholds the other two councils and thereby detaches them from their foundation.

---

[1] *Thesen zum Thema 'Zehn Jahre Vaticanum II'*, 1f. Typewritten manuscript.
[2] Ibid.

And this applies to the so-called 'traditionalism', also in its extreme forms." "Every partisan choice destroys the whole (the very history of the Church) which can exist only as an indivisible unity."[3]

Let us rediscover the true Vatican II

Hence it is not Vatican II and its documents (it is hardly necessary to recall this) that are problematic. At all events, many see the problem—and Joseph Ratzinger is among them, and not just since yesterday—to lie in the manifold interpretations of those documents which have led to many abuses in the post-conciliar period.

Ratzinger's judgment on this period has been clearly formulated for a long time: "It is incontestable that the last ten years have been decidedly unfavorable for the Catholic Church."[4] "Developments since the Council seem to be in striking contrast to the expectations of all, beginning with those of John XXIII and Paul VI. Christians are once again a minority, more than they have ever been since the end of antiquity."

He explains his stark judgment (which he also repeated during the interview—but that should not cause any surprise, whatever judgment we might make of it, for he confirmed it many times) as follows: "What the Popes and the Council Fathers were expecting was a new Catholic unity, and instead one has encountered a dissension which—to use the words of Paul VI—seems to have passed over from self-criticism to self-destruction. There had been the expectation of a new enthusiasm, and instead too often it has ended in

---

[3] Ibid. Contains insertions in (Messori's) manuscript.
[4] *Thesen zum Thema 'Zehn Jahre Vaticanum II'*, 1f.

boredom and discouragement. There had been the expectation of a step forward, and instead one found oneself facing a progressive process of decadence that to a large measure has been unfolding under the sign of a summons to a presumed 'spirit of the Council' and by so doing has actually and increasingly discredited it."

Thus, already ten years ago, he had arrived at the following conclusion: "It must be clearly stated that a real reform of the Church presupposes an unequivocal turning away from the erroneous paths whose catastrophic consequences are already incontestable."

On one occasion he also wrote: "Cardinal Julius Döpfner once remarked that the Church of the post-conciliar period is a huge construction site. But a critical spirit later added that it was a construction site where the blueprint had been lost and everyone continues to build according to his taste. The result is evident."

Nevertheless the Cardinal constantly takes pains to repeat, with equal clarity, that "Vatican II in its official promulgations, in its authentic documents, cannot be held responsible for this development which, on the contrary, radically contradicts both the letter and the spirit of the Council Fathers."

He says: "I am convinced that the damage that we have incurred in these twenty years is due, not to the 'true' Council, but to the unleashing *within* the Church of latent polemical and centrifugal forces; and *outside* the Church it is due to the confrontation with a cultural revolution in the West: the success of the upper middle class, the new 'tertiary bourgeoisie', with its liberal–radical ideology of individualistic, rationalistic and hedonistic stamp."

Hence his message, his exhortation to all Catholics who wish to remain such, is certainly not to "*turn back*" but, rather, "to *return to the authentic texts of the original Vatican II*".

For him, he repeats to me, "to defend the true tradition of the Church today means to defend the Council. It is also our fault if we have at times provided a pretext (to the 'right' and 'left' alike) to view Vatican II as a 'break' and an abandonment of the tradition. There is, instead, a continuity that allows neither a return to the past nor a flight forward, neither anachronistic longings nor unjustified impatience. We must remain faithful to the *today* of the Church, not the *yesterday* or *tomorrow*. And this today of the Church is the documents of Vatican II, without *reservations* that amputate them and without *arbitrariness* that distorts them."

A prescription against anachronism

Although critical of the "left", Ratzinger also exhibits an unmistakable severity toward the "right", toward that integralist traditionalism quintessentially symbolized by the old Archbishop Marcel Lefebvre. In a reference to it, he told me: "I see no future for a position that, out of principle, stubbornly renounces Vatican II. In fact in itself it is an illogical position. The point of departure for this tendency is, in fact, the strictest fidelity to the teaching particularly of Pius IX and Pius X and, still more fundamentally, of Vatican I and its definition of papal primacy. But why only the popes up to Pius XII and not beyond? Is perhaps obedience to the Holy See divisible according to years or according to the nearness of a teaching to one's own already-established convictions?"

The fact remains, I observe, that if Rome has intervened with respect to the "left", it has not yet intervened with respect to the "right" with the same vigor.

In reply, he states: "The followers of Msgr. Lefebvre assert the very opposite. They contend that whereas there was an immediate intervention in the case of the respected retired Archbishop with the harsh punishment of suspension, there is an incomprehensible toleration of every kind of deviation from the other side. I don't wish to get involved in a polemic on the greater or lesser severity toward the one or the other side. Besides, both types of opposition present entirely different features. The deviation toward the 'left' no doubt represents a broad current of the contemporary thought and action of the Church, but hardly anywhere have they found a juridically definable common form. On the other hand, Archbishop Lefebvre's movement is probably much less broad numerically, but it has a well-defined juridical organization, seminaries, religious houses, etc. Clearly everything possible must be done to prevent this movement from giving rise to a schism peculiar to it that would come into being whenever Msgr. Lefebvre should decide to consecrate a bishop which, thank God, in the hope of a reconciliation, he has not yet done. In the ecumenical sphere today one deplores that not enough was done in the past to prevent incipient divisions through a greater openness to reconciliation and to an understanding of the different groups. Well, that should apply as a behavioral maxim for us too in the present time. We must commit ourselves to reconciliation, so long and so far as it is possible, and we must utilize all the opportunities granted to us for this purpose."

But Lefebvre, I object, has ordained priests and continues to do so.

"Canon law speaks of ordinations that are illicit but not invalid. We must also consider the human aspect of these young men who, in the eyes of the Church, are 'true'

priests, albeit in an irregular situation. The point of departure and the orientation of individuals are certainly different. Some are strongly influenced by their family situations
and have accepted the latter's decision. In others, disillu-
sionment with the present-day Church has driven them to
bitterness and to negation. Others still would like to col-
laborate fully in the normal pastoral activity of the Church.
Nevertheless they have let themselves be driven to their
choice by the unsatisfactory situation that has arisen in the
seminaries in many countries. So just as there are some who
in some way have put up with the division, there are also
many who hope for reconciliation and remain in Msgr.
Lefebvre's priestly community only in this hope."

His prescription for cutting the ground from under the
Lefebvre case and other anachronistic resistances seems to
reecho that of the last popes, from Paul VI to today:
"Similar absurd situations have been able to endure up to
now precisely by nourishing themselves on the arbitrariness
and thoughtlessness of many post-conciliar interpretations.
This places a further obligation upon us to show the true
face of the Council: thus one will be able to cut the ground
from under these false protests."

Spirit and anti-spirit

But, I say, opinions differ as regard the "true" Council.
Apart from the cases of that irresponsible "neo-trium-
phalism" to which you referred and which refuses to look at
reality, there is general agreement that the present situation
of the Church is a difficult one. But opinions come to a part-
ing of the ways with respect to diagnosis as well as therapy.
The *diagnosis* of some is that the appearances of crisis are only

the salutary fevers of a period of growth. For others, instead, they are symptoms of a grave illness. As regards the *therapy*, some demand a greater application of Vatican II, even beyond the texts. Others propose a minor dose of reforms and changes. How to choose? Who is to be declared right?

He answers: "As I shall explain in great detail, my diagnosis is that we are dealing with an authentic crisis and that it must be treated and cured. Thus, I confirm that even for this healing process, Vatican II is a reality that must be fully accepted. On condition, however, that it must not be viewed as merely a point of departure from which one gets further away by running forward, but as a base on which to build solidly. Today, in fact, we are discovering its 'prophetic' function: some texts of Vatican II at the moment of their proclamation seemed really to be ahead of the times. Then came the cultural revolutions and the social convulsions that the Fathers in no way could have foreseen but which have shown how their answers — at that time anticipatory — were those that were needed in the future. Hence it is obvious that return to the documents is of special importance at the present time: they give us the right instrument with which to face the problems of our day. We are summoned to reconstruct the Church, not *despite*, but *thanks* to the true Council."

Continuing his diagnosis, he recalls that this "true" Council, "already during its sessions and then increasingly in the subsequent period, was opposed by a self-styled 'spirit of the Council', which in reality is a true 'anti-spirit' of the Council. According to this pernicious anti-spirit [*Konzils-Ungeist* in German], everything that is 'new' (or presumed such: how many old heresies have surfaced again in recent years that have been presented as something new!) is always and in every case better than what has been or what is. It is the anti-spirit according to which the history of the Church would first begin with Vatican II, viewed as a kind of point zero."

"Not rupture but continuity"

On this point, he insists, he wants to be very precise. "This schematism of a *before* and *after* in the history of the Church, wholly unjustified by the documents of Vatican II, which do nothing but reaffirm the continuity of Catholicism, must be decidedly opposed. There is no 'pre-' or 'post-' conciliar Church: there is but one, unique Church that walks the path toward the Lord, ever deepening and ever better understanding the treasure of faith that he himself has entrusted to her. There are no leaps in this history, there are no fractures, and there is no break in continuity. In no wise did the Council intend to introduce a temporal dichotomy in the Church."

Continuing his analysis, he recalls that "in no way was it the intention of the pope who took the initiative for Vatican II, John XXIII, and of the pope who continued it faithfully, Paul VI, to bring up for discussion a *depositum fidei* which was viewed by them as undisputed and already assured."

Do you wish, perhaps, as some do, to stress the primarily *pastoral* concerns of Vatican II?

"I should like to say that Vatican II surely did not want 'to change' the faith, but to represent it in a more effective way. Further, I should say that dialogue is possible only on the foundation of a clear identity. One can, one must be 'open', but only when one has something to say and has acquired one's own identity. This is how the Popes and the Council Fathers understood it. Some of them no doubt harbored an optimism that from our present-day perspective we would judge as not critical or realistic enough. But if they thought that they could open themselves with confidence to what is positive in the modern world, it was precisely because they were sure of their identity, of their faith. Whereas on the part of many Catholics in recent years there has been an unrestrained and unfiltered opening to the world, that is to say, to the dominant modern mentality, which at the same time brings up for discussion the very foundations of the *depositum fidei* which for many were no longer clear."

He continues: "Vatican II was right in its desire for a revision of the relations between the Church and the world. There are in fact values, which, even though they originated outside the Church, can find their place—provided they are clarified and corrected—in her perspective. This task has been accomplished in these years. But whoever thinks that these two realities can meet each other without conflict or even be identical would betray that he understands neither the Church nor the world."

Are you proposing, perhaps, a return to the old spirit of "opposition to the world"?

"It is not Christians who oppose the world, but rather the world which opposes itself to them when the truth about God, about Christ and about man is proclaimed. The world waxes indignant when sin and grace are called by their names. After the phase of indiscriminate 'openness' it is time that the Christian reacquire the consciousness of belonging to a minority and of often being in opposition to what is obvious, plausible and natural for that mentality which the New Testament calls—and certainly not in a positive sense—the 'spirit of the world'. It is time to find again the courage of nonconformism, the capacity to oppose many of the trends of the surrounding culture, renouncing a certain euphoric post-conciliar solidarity."

Restoration?

At this point — here, too, as during the whole interview, the tape recorder whirred in the silence of the room overlooking the seminary garden — I posed to Cardinal Ratzinger the question whose answer aroused the liveliest reactions. Reactions which were also due to the incomplete ways in which it has often been reported, as well as to the emotion-laden content of the word involved ("restoration"), which hearkens back to times long past and which are certainly neither repeatable nor — at least in our view — even desirable.

Accordingly I asked the Prefect of the Congregation for the Faith: "Considering what you are saying, it would seem that those who assert that the Church hierarchy intends to close the first phase of the post-conciliar period are not wrong. And that (even though it certainly would not be a return to the pre-conciliar period but to the 'authentic' documents of Vatican II) the same hierarchy intends to set a kind of 'restoration' in motion."

This is the Cardinal's reply, in his own words: "If by 'restoration' is meant a turning back, no restoration of such kind is possible. The Church moves forward toward the consummation of history, she looks ahead to the Lord who is coming. No, there is no going back, nor is it possible to go back. Hence there is no 'restoration' whatsoever in this sense. But if by *restoration* we understand the search for a new balance after all the exaggerations of an indiscriminate opening to the world, after the overly positive interpretations of an agnostic and atheistic world, well, then a *restoration* understood in this sense (a newly found balance of orientations and values within the Catholic totality) is altogether desirable and, for that matter, is already in operation in the Church. In this sense it can be said that the first phase after Vatican II has come to a close."[5]

Unforeseen effects

In his view, as he explains to me, "the situation has changed, the climate has changed for the worse with respect to that which sustained a euphoria whose fruits now lie before us as a warning. The Christian is held to that *realism* which is

[5] In many press comments on this reply, the term "restoration" has not been grasped with all its necessary precisions as reported here. Consequently, queried by a newspaper, Cardinal Ratzinger stated the following in a letter: "Above all I should simply like to recall what I really said: there is no return to the past. A restoration understood thus is not only impossible but also not even desirable. The Church moves forward to the consummation of history, she looks ahead to the Lord who is coming. If, however, the term 'restoration' is understood according to its semantic content, that is to say, as a recovery of lost values, within a new totality, then I would like to say that this is precisely the task that imposes itself today in the second phase of the post-conciliar period. Yet the word 'restoration' is linguistically laden in such a way for us moderns that it is difficult to attribute this meaning to it. In reality it literally means the same as the word 'reform', a term that has a wholly different sound to us today. Perhaps I can clarify the matter with an example taken from history. For me Charles Borromeo is the classic expression of a real reform, that is to say, of a renewal that leads forward precisely because it teaches how to live the permanent values in a new way, bearing in mind the totality of the Christian fact and the totality of man.

"It can certainly be said that Charles Borromeo rebuilt ('restored') the Catholic Church, which also in the area around Milan was at that time nearly destroyed for awhile, without making a return to the Middle Ages. On the contrary, he created a modern form of the Church. How little 'restorative' such a reform was is seen, for example, in the fact that

nothing but complete attention to the signs of the times. Therefore I exclude the possibility that any thought can be given (unrealistically) to go back along the road as if Vatican II had never been. Many of the concrete effects, as we see them now, do not correspond to the intentions of the Council Fathers, but we certainly cannot say: 'It would have been better if it had not been'. John Henry Cardinal Newman, the historian of the councils, the great scholar who was converted to Catholicism from Anglicanism, said that a council was always a risk for the Church and that, consequently, it should only be called to discuss a limited number of issues and not be overly protracted. True, reforms require time, patience, and a readiness to take risks,

---

Charles suppressed a religious order that was nearly in decline and assigned its goods to new, live communities. Who today possesses a similar courage to declare that that which is interiorly dead (and continues to live only exteriorly) belongs definitively to the past and must be entrusted with clarity to the energies of the new era? Often new phenomena of Christian awakening are resisted precisely by the so-called reformers, who in their turn spasmodically defend institutions that continue to exist only in contradiction with themselves

"In Charles Borromeo, therefore, we can also see what I meant to say with 'reform' or 'restoration' in its original meaning: to live outstretched toward a totality, to live from a 'yes' that leads back to the unity of the human forces in conflict with each other. A 'yes' that confers on them a positive meaning within the totality. In Charles Borromeo we can also see the essential prerequisite for a similar renewal. Charles could convince others because he himself was a man of conviction. He was able to exist with his certitudes amid the contradictions of his time because he himself lived them. And he could live them because he was a Christian in the deepest sense of the word, in other words, he was totally centered on Christ. What truly counts is to reestablish this all-embracing relation to Christ. No one can be convinced of this all-embracing relationship to Christ through argumentation alone. One can live it, however, and thereby make it credible to others and invite others to share it."

but it is still not permissible to say: 'Let's not convoke councils because they are dangerous.' I believe, rather, that the true time of Vatican II has not yet come, that its authentic reception has not yet begun: its documents were quickly buried under a pile of superficial or frankly inexact publications. The reading of the *letter* of the documents will enable us to discover their true *spirit*. If thus rediscovered in their truth, those great texts will make it possible for us to understand just what happened and to react with a new vigor. I repeat: the Catholic who clearly and, consequently, painfully perceives the damage that has been wrought in his Church by the misinterpretations of Vatican II must find the possibility of revival in Vatican II itself. The Council is *his,* it does not belong to those who want to continue along a road whose results have been catastrophic. It does not belong to those, who, not by chance, don't know just what to make of Vatican II, which they look upon as a 'fossil of the clerical era'."

It has been remarked, I say, that Vatican II is an *unicum* also because it was, perhaps, the first council in history to be convoked, not under the pressure of pressing problems or crises, but in a moment of seeming tranquility with respect to ecclesial life. The crises erupted later, not only within the Church but in the whole society. Could it not be said (to return, moreover, to one of your previous indications) that the Church, at all events, would have had to confront those cultural revolutions but that, without the Council, her structure would have been more rigid and the damages could have possibly been even more grave? Has not her more flexible and more elastic post-conciliar structure, perhaps, been better able to absorb the impact, even though she nonetheless has to foot the necessary bill?

"It's impossible to say", he replies. "History, above all the history of the Church which God leads along mysterious paths, is not made of 'ifs'. We must accept it as it is. At the beginning of the sixties, the post-war generation began to appear on the scene, that generation which had not directly participated in the reconstruction, which found an already-reconstructed world and therefore was seeking elsewhere for motives for commitment, for renewal. There was a general atmosphere of optimism and faith in progress. Moreover, everybody in the Church shared the expectation of a tranquil further development of her doctrine. It must not be forgotten that my predecessor in the Holy Office, Cardinal Ottaviani, also supported the project of an ecumenical council. After Pope John XXIII had announced its convocation, the Roman Curia worked together with the most distinguished representatives of the world episcopate in the preparation of those schemata which were then rejected by the Council Fathers as too theoretical, too textbook-like and insufficiently pastoral. Pope John had not reckoned on the possibility of a rejection but was expecting a quick and frictionless balloting on these projects which he had approvingly read. It is clear that none of those texts aimed to change doctrine. Rather, it was a matter of synthesizing it, at most, of arriving also at a clarification of some points not yet precisely defined and, in that way, of developing it further. Even the rejection of these texts by the Council Fathers was not directed against the doctrine as such, but against the inadequate way of expressing it and certainly also against some definitions that had never existed up to then and are considered unnecessary even today.

"What is certain is that the Council did not take the turn that John XXIII had expected (let us recall that countries like Holland, Switzerland and the United States were strongholds of traditionalism and loyalty to Rome!). It must also be admitted that, in respect to the whole Church, the prayer of Pope John that the Council signify a new leap forward for the Church, to renewed life and unity, has not—at least not yet—been granted."

The hope of the "movements"

But, I ask, worried, doesn't your negative view of the reality of the post-conciliar Church leave any room for some positive element?

"Paradoxically", he answers, "it is precisely the negative that can be changed to positive in the first instance. Many Catholics, in recent years, have experienced the Exodus; they have seen the results of conformism to ideologies; they have learned what it means to await redemption, freedom, hope from the world. Up to now what aspect a life without God, a world without faith, would assume was known only in theory. Now it has been ascertained in reality. Starting out from this emptiness, we can newly discover the richness of the faith, its indispensability. For many, these years have been like an arduous purification, almost a path through fire, that has opened the possibility of a deeper faith."

"It must not be forgotten", he continues, "that every council is first of all a reform of the 'summit' which then must spread to the base of the faithful. This means that every council, in order really to yield fruit, must be followed by a wave of holiness. Thus it was after Trent, and it achieved its aim of real reform precisely for this reason. Salvation for the Church comes from within her, but this in no way means to say that it comes from the decrees of the hierarchy. Whether Vatican II and its results will be considered as a luminous period of Church history will depend upon all the Catholics who are called to give it life. As John Paul II said in his

commemoration of Borromeo in Milan: 'the Church of today does not need any new reformers. The Church needs
new saints'."

So you don't see, I insist, any other positive signs—except for those that come from the "negative"—in this
period of Church history?

"Of course I see them. I will not speak here of the
momentum of the young churches (like that of South
Korea) or of the vitality of the persecuted churches because
that cannot immediately be traced back to Vatican II. Just as
the crisis phenomena cannot be directly attributed to it.
What is hopeful at the level of the universal Church—and
that is happening right in the heart of the crisis of the
Church in the Western world—is the rise of new movements which nobody had planned and which nobody has
called into being, but which have sprung spontaneously
from the inner vitality of the faith itself. What is manifested
in them—albeit subdued—is something like a pentecostal
season in the Church. I am thinking, say, of the charismatic
movement, of the Cursillos, of the movement of the
Focolare, of the neo-catechumenal communities, of Communion and Liberation, etc. Certainly all these movements
also give rise to some problems. They also entail greater or
lesser dangers. But that happens with all living beings. I am
now, to an increasing degree, meeting groups of young
people in whom there is a wholehearted adhesion to the
whole faith of the Church, young people who want to live
this faith fully and who bear in themselves a great missionary élan. The intense life of prayer present in these
movements does not imply a flight into interiority or a
withdrawal into the private sphere, but simply a full and
undivided catholicity. The joy of the faith that one senses
here has something contagious about it. Here new vocations

to the priesthood and to the religious orders are now growing spontaneously.

"What is striking is that all this fervor was not elaborated by any office of pastoral planning, but somehow it sprang forth by itself. As a consequence of this fact, the planning offices—just when they want to be very progressive—don't know just what to do with them. They don't fit into their plan. Thus while tensions rise in connection with their incorporation into the present form of the institutions, there is absolutely no tension with the hierarchical Church as such.

"What is emerging here is a new generation of the Church which I am watching with a great hope. I find it marvelous that the Spirit is once more stronger than our programs and brings himself into play in an altogether different way than we had imagined. In this sense the renewal, in a subdued but effective way, is afoot. Old forms that had run aground in self-contradiction and in the taste for negation are leaving the stage, and the new is making headway. Naturally it does not yet have its full voice in the great debate of dominant ideas. It grows in silence. Our task—the task of the office-holders in the Church and of theologians—is to keep the door open to them, to prepare room for them. For the present, still prevalent trends are in fact moving in an altogether different direction. If one looks directly at the 'general meteorological situation' of the Spirit, we must speak, as we did earlier, of a crisis of faith and of the Church. We can overcome it only if we face up to it forthrightly."

CHAPTER THREE

AT THE ROOT OF THE CRISIS: THE IDEA OF CHURCH

The façade and the mystery

So, it's a *crisis*. But where, in your opinion, is the principal point of rupture, the crack which, by widening, threatens the stability of the whole edifice of the Catholic faith?

No doubts exist in Cardinal Ratzinger's mind: the alarm must focus before all else on the crisis of the understanding of the Church, on ecclesiology: "Herein lies the cause of a good part of the misunderstandings or real errors which endanger theology and common Catholic opinion alike."

He explains: "My impression is that the authentically Catholic meaning of the reality 'Church' is tacitly disappearing, without being expressly rejected. Many no longer believe that what is at issue is a reality willed by the Lord himself. Even with some theologians, the Church appears to be a human construction, an instrument created by us and one which we ourselves can freely reorganize according to the requirements of the moment. In other words, in many ways a conception of Church is spreading in Catholic thought, and even in Catholic theology, that cannot even be called Protestant in a 'classic' sense. Many current ecclesiological ideas, rather, refer to the model of certain North

American 'free churches', in which in the past believers took refuge from the oppressive model of the 'State Church' produced by the Reformation. Those refugees, no longer believing in an institutional Church willed by Christ, and wanting at the same time to escape the State Church, created their *own* church, an organization structured according to their needs."

How is it with Catholics instead?

"For a Catholic", he explains, "the Church is indeed composed of men who organize her external visage. But behind this, the fundamental structures are willed by God himself, and therefore they are inviolable. Behind the *human* exterior stands the mystery of a *more than human* reality, in which reformers, sociologists, organizers have no authority whatsoever. If the Church, instead, is viewed as a human construction, the product of our own efforts, even the contents of the faith end up assuming an arbitrary character: the faith, in fact, no longer has an authentic, guaranteed instrument through which to express itself. Thus, without a view of the mystery of the Church that is also *supernatural* and not only *sociological,* christology itself loses its reference to the divine in favor of a purely human structure, and ultimately it amounts to a purely human project: the Gospel becomes the *Jesus-project*, the social-liberation project or other merely historical, immanent projects that can still seem religious in appearance, but which are atheistic in substance."

During Vatican II there was a great emphasis—in the interventions of some bishops, in the statements of their theological advisers, but also in the final documents—on the concept of the Church as "People of God", a conception which subsequently seemed to dominate in the post-conciliar ecclesiologies.

"That's true. There was and there still is this emphasis,

which in the Council texts, however, is balanced with others that complete it. A balance that has been lost with many theologians. Yet, contrary to what the latter think, in this way there is the risk of moving backward rather than forward. Here indeed there is even the danger of abandoning the New Testament in order to return to the Old. 'People of God' in Scripture, in fact, is a reference to Israel in its relationship of prayer and fidelity to the Lord. But to limit the definition of the Church to that expression means not to give expression to the New Testament understanding of the Church in its fullness. Here 'People of God' actually refers always to the Old Testament element of the Church, to her continuity with Israel. But the Church receives her New Testament character more distinctively in the concept of the 'Body of Christ'. One is Church and one is a member thereof, not through a sociological adherence, but precisely through incorporation in this Body of the Lord through baptism and the Eucharist. Behind the concept of the Church as the People of God, which has been so exclusively thrust into the foreground today, hide influences of ecclesiologies which de facto revert to the Old Testament; and perhaps also political, partisan and collectivist influences. In reality, there is no truly New Testament, Catholic concept of Church without a direct and vital relation not only with sociology but first of all with christology. The Church does not exhaust herself in the 'collective' of the believers: being the 'Body of Christ' she is much more than the simple sum of her members."

For the Prefect, the gravity of the situation is accentuated by the fact that—on so vital a point as ecclesiology—it does not seem possible to bring about a clarification through promulgations. And although these have not been lacking, in his view what would be necessary is a work in depth. "It is necessary to recreate an authentically *Catholic* climate, to find again the meaning of the Church as Church of the Lord, as the locus of the real presence of God in the world. That mystery of which Vatican II speaks when it writes those awesomely challenging words which correspond nonetheless to the whole Catholic tradition: 'the Church, or, in other words, *the Kingdom of Christ now present in mystery*' " (*Lumen Gentium*, no. 3).

"It is not ours, it is his"

In confirmation of the "qualitative" difference of the Church with respect to any other human organization whatsoever, he recalls that "only the Church, in this world, goes beyond even the radically impassable frontier: the frontier of death. Living or dead, the members of the Church live in association with the same life that proceeds from the incorporation of all in the Body of Christ."

It is the reality, I observe, that Catholic theology has always called *communio sanctorum*, the communion of "saints", in which all the baptized are "saints".

"Of course", he says. "But it must not be forgotten that the Latin expression does not mean only the union of the members of the Church, living or dead. *Communio sanctorum* means also to have 'holy things' in common, that is to say, the grace of the sacraments that pours forth from the dead and resurrected Christ. It is precisely this mysterious yet real bond, this union in Life, that is also the reason why the Church is not *our* Church, which we could dispose of as we please. She is, rather, *his* Church. All that which is only *our* Church is not Church in the deep sense; it belongs to her human—hence secondary, transitory—aspect."

Does the modern forgetfulness or rejection of this Catholic concept of the Church, I ask, not also involve consequences in the relation with the ecclesial hierarchy?

"Certainly. And among the gravest. Here lies the origin of the decline of the authentic concept of 'obedience'. According to some it would no longer even be a Christian virtue but a heritage of an authoritarian, dogmatic past, hence one to be overcome. If the Church, in fact, is *our* Church, if *we alone* are the Church, if her structures are not willed by Christ, then it is no longer possible to conceive of the existence of a hierarchy as a service to the baptized established by the Lord himself. It is a rejection of the concept of an authority willed by God, an authority therefore that has its legitimation in God and not—as happens in political structures—in the consensus of the majority of the members of an organization. But the Church of Christ is not a party, not an association, not a club. Her deep and permanent structure is not *democratic* but *sacramental*, consequently *hierarchical*. For the hierarchy based on the apostolic succession is the indispensable condition to arrive at the strength, the reality of the sacrament. Here authority is not based on the majority of votes; it is based on the authority of Christ himself, which he willed to pass on to men who were to be his representatives until his definitive return. Only if this perspective is acquired anew will it be possible to rediscover the necessity and fruitfulness of obedience to the legitimate ecclesiastical hierarchies."

For a real reform

Yet alongside the traditional expression *communio sanctorum* (in that comprehensive meaning), I remark, there is also another Latin phrase that has always enjoyed validity among Catholics: *Ecclesia semper reformanda*, the Church is always needful of reform. The Council has clearly expressed itself on this score:

"By the power of the Holy Spirit the Church is the faithful spouse of the Lord and will never fail to be a sign of salvation in the world; but she is by no means unaware that down through the centuries there have been among her members, both clerical and lay, some who were disloyal to the Spirit of God. Today as well, the Church is not blind to the discrepancy between the message she proclaims and the human weakness of those to whom the Gospel has been entrusted. Whatever is history's judgment on these shortcomings, we cannot ignore them and we must combat them earnestly, lest they hinder the spread of the Gospel" (*Gaudium et spes*, no. 43).

Even respecting the mystery are we not also called to make efforts to change the Church?

"To be sure", he replies, "in her human structures the Church is *semper reformanda*, but one must be clear in this question as to how and up to what point. The text cited from Vatican II already gives a quite precise indication, by speaking of the 'fidelity of the Bride of Christ' which is not called in question by the infidelities of her members. But in order to make this clearer, I shall refer to the Latin formula which the Roman liturgy had the celebrant pronounce in every Mass, at the 'sign of peace' preceding communion. That prayer read: *Domine Jesu Christe . . . Ne respicias peccata mea, sed fidem Ecclesiae tuae*. That is to say: 'Lord Jesus Christ, look not upon *my* sins, but upon the faith of *your* Church'. Now in many translations of the Ordinary of the Mass into the language of different countries (but also in the renewed Latin text), the formula has been changed from this 'I' form to a 'We' form: 'Look not upon *our* sins'. A change of this kind may appear irrelevant at first, but it is of great significance."

Why attribute such importance to the change from I to We?

"Because", he explains, "the use of the singular is an allusion to the necessity of a *personal* admission of one's own fault, to the requisiteness of *personal* conversion which today is very often hidden in the anonymous mass of 'We', of the group, of the 'system', of humanity. Hence, in the end, where all have sinned, nobody seems to have sinned. In this way the sense of personal responsibility, of the faults of each one, is dissolved. Naturally the new version of the text can be understood in a correct manner, because the *I* and the *We* are always intertwined in sin—and, of course, in the Lords prayer itself we pray, 'Forgive us *our* trespasses'. But the alteration here does nevertheless reinforce the contemporary tendency to diminish personal responsibility. What is important is that in the new emphasis on the We, the I not disappear."

This point, I remark, is important, and it will be worthwhile to come back to it later. But for the moment let us go back where we were: to the connection between the axiom *Ecclesia semper reformanda* and the invocation to Christ for personal forgiveness.

"Agreed, let us go back to that prayer which liturgical wisdom inserted at the most solemn moment of the Mass, to that moment of physical, intimate union with Christ who has transformed himself into bread and wine. The Church presumed that anyone who celebrated the Eucharist would need to say: *I* have sinned, Lord, look not upon *my* sins. It was the obligatory invocation of every priest: each bishop, the pope himself like the least priest had to pronounce it in his daily Mass. And also the laity, all the other members of the Church, were called to unite themselves to that recognition of guilt. Therefore, *everybody* in the Church, with no exception, had to confess himself to be a sinner, beseech forgiveness and then set out on the path of his real reform. But this in no way means that the Church as such was also a sinner. The Church — as we have seen — is a reality that surpasses, mysteriously and infinitely, the sum of her members. In fact, in order to obtain Christ's forgiveness, *my sin* was set over against the *faith of his Church.*"

And today?

"Today this seems to have been forgotten by many theologians, priests and laymen. It is not only the change from the *I* to the *We*, from personal to collective responsibility. One even gets the impression that some, although unconsciously, may reverse the prayer by understanding it in this way: 'Look not upon the *sins of the Church* but upon *my faith. . .*' Should this really happen, the consequences will be grave: the faults of individuals become the faults of the Church, and faith is reduced to a personal event, to *my* way of understanding and of accepting God and his demands. I really fear that today this is a widespread manner of feeling and thinking. It is another sign of how greatly in many places the common Catholic consciousness has distanced itself from an authentic conception of the Church."

What is to be done, then?

"We must", he replies, "go back to saying to the Lord: 'We sin, but the Church that is yours and the bearer of faith does not sin.' Faith is the answer of the Church to Christ. It is Church in the measure that it is an act of faith. This faith is not an individual, solitary act, a response of the individual. Faith means to believe *together*, with all the Church."

Where, then, can those "reforms" that we are always

enjoined to introduce to our community of believers, who live in history, address themselves?

He says, "We must always bear in mind that the Church is not ours but his. Hence the 'reform', the 'renewals' — necessary as they may be — cannot exhaust themselves in a zealous activity on our part to erect new, sophisticated structures. The most that can come from a work of this kind is a Church that is 'ours', to our measure, which might indeed be interesting but which, by itself, is nevertheless not the true Church, that which sustains us with the faith and gives us life with the sacrament. I mean to say that what we can do is infinitely inferior to him who does. Hence, true 'reform' does not mean to take great pains to erect new façades (contrary to what certain ecclesiologies think). Real 'reform' is to strive to let what is ours disappear as much as possible so what belongs to Christ may become more visible. It is a truth well known to the saints. Saints, in fact, reformed the Church in depth, not by working up plans for new structures, but by reforming themselves. What the Church needs in order to respond to the needs of man in every age is holiness, not management."

CHAPTER FOUR

AMONG PRIESTS AND BISHOPS

Priest: a man of inquietude

If the very concept of "Church" is in crisis, to what extent and why are the "*men of the Church*" in crisis?

Postponing a discussion on the episcopate, which will follow later in this same chapter, where does Ratzinger see the roots of a clerical restlessness which in the space of a few years has emptied seminaries, convents, presbyteries? In a recent unofficial talk, he quoted the thesis of a famous theologian according to whom "the crisis of the Church today is before all else a crisis of priests and religious orders".

"It is a harsh judgment," he confirms, "a rather grim *J'accuse*, but maybe it has grasped a truth. Under the onslaught of the post-conciliar period, the great religious orders (in other words, precisely the traditional pillars of the ever-necessary ecclesial reform) have vacillated, have undergone grave hemorrhages and have seen new admissions reduced to levels never experienced before, and they still seem to be shaken by an identity crisis."

Indeed, in his view, "it has often been the traditionally most 'educated', the intellectually best equipped orders that have undergone the gravest crises." And he perceives one of the reasons for it: "Whoever has practiced and practices a certain contemporary theology, lives its consequences to the utmost, as the almost complete loss of the usual certitudes that marked the priest, the religious."

To this first reason for the crisis, the Prefect adds another: "The very situation of the priest is singular, alien to modern society. A function, a role that is not based on the consent of the majority but on the representation of *another* who lets a man share his authority appears as something incomprehensible. Under these conditions there is a great temptation to pass from that supernatural 'authority of representation', the hallmark of Catholic priesthood, to a much more natural 'service of the coordination of consensus', that is to say, to a comprehensible category, because it is only human and, besides, more in consonance with modern culture."

So, if I have properly understood, in your view the priesthood is being exposed to a cultural pressure that would have it pass from a "sacral" role to a "social" role, in line with the "democratic" mechanisms of consensus formation from below that mark the "secular, democratic pluralist society"?

"Something of the kind", he confirms. "It is, so to speak," he replies, "a temptation to flee from the mystery of the hierarchical structure founded by Christ toward the more plausible character of human organization."

In order to make his point of view clearer, he resorts to an example of great topical interest, the sacrament of reconciliation, confession. "There are priests who tend to transform it almost exclusively into a 'conversation', into a kind of therapeutic self-analysis between two persons on the same level. That seems to be much more human, more personal and more adapted to modern man. But this kind of confession incurs the risk of having little to do with the Catholic conception of the sacrament, where the performance, the ability of the person entrusted with the office are not of such great import. Rather it is much more necessary that the priest be willing to remain in the background, thus leaving space for Christ, who alone can remit sin. Even here it is therefore necessary to return to the authentic context of the sacrament, where men encounter mystery. The sense of the scandal through which a man can say to another man, 'I absolve you from your sins', must be rediscovered. In that moment — as happens for that matter in every other sacrament — the priest certainly does not draw his authority from the consent of men but directly from Christ. The 'I' that says: 'I absolve you' is not that of a creature, but it is directly the 'I' of the Lord."

Nevertheless, I say, the many criticisms of the "old" way of making confession do not seem to be wholly groundless. He instantly replies: "I feel increasingly uneasy when I hear the once widespread manner of approaching the confessional so lightly defined as 'repetitious', 'external' and 'anonymous'. And for me the self-praise of some priests for their 'penitential colloquies', which have become infrequent but, as they say, 'in compensation, much more personal', has an increasingly bitter ring in my ear. Viewed properly, behind the 'repetitiousness' of certain confessions of the past, there was also the seriousness of the encounter between two persons aware of being in the presence of the shattering mystery of Christ's forgiveness that arrives through the words and gestures of a sinful man. Nor should it be forgotten that in so many 'colloquies' that have become quite analytical, it is human that a kind of complacency, a self-absolution should creep in which — in the flood of explanations — almost leaves no further room for the sense of personal sin, for which, beyond all attenuating circumstances, we are always responsible. I don't mean to say that there could not also be a meaningful reform of the external celebration of confession. Here history shows such a breadth of developments that it

would be absurd to want to canonize forever a single form,
the present one. Undoubtedly many persons today no longer
manage to find access to the traditional confessional, whereas the colloquy really opens a door for them. Hence I would
not in any way underestimate the importance of these new
possibilities and the blessing that they can represent for
many. But this is not the fundamental question. The decisive point of the question lies deeper, and I wanted to
point to it."

Returning to what for him is the source of the crisis of
the priest, he speaks of the "pressure that every moment
weighs heavily upon a man such as today's priest, who is so
often called to swim against the current. Such a man, in the
end, can grow weary of resisting, with his words and even
more with his life-style, the seemingly so reasonable realities
that are accepted as a matter of course and that characterize
our culture. The priest—the one, that is, through whom
the strength of the Lord passes—has always been tempted to
habituate himself to this greatness, to let it become routine.
Today he could experience the greatness of the Sacred as a
burden and long (even unconsciously) to free himself from
it, lowering the mystery to his human stature, instead of
abandoning himself to it with humility but with trust, so as
to lift himself up to that height."

The problem of episcopal conferences

From "simple" priests we now pass to bishops, that is, to
those who, being "successors of the apostles", hold the "fullness of the sacrament of orders". They are "authentic teachers" of the Christian doctrine who enjoy "ordinary, autonomous and immediate authority in the dioceses entrusted to

them" of which they are the "principle and foundation of unity". United in the episcopal college with their head, the pope, "they act in the person of Christ" in order to govern the universal Church.

All these definitions that we have given are peculiar to Catholic doctrine on the episcopate, and they have been vigorously reaffirmed by Vatican II.

"The Council", recalls Cardinal Ratzinger, "wanted specifically to strengthen the role and responsibility of bishops by resuming and completing the work, interrupted by the capture of Rome, of Vatican I, which was only able to concern itself with the pope. The Council Fathers had confirmed the latter's infallibility in the Magisterium when, as supreme Shepherd and Teacher, he proclaims a teaching on faith or on morals as binding."

By so doing, a certain imbalance was created with some theologians who did not sufficiently stress that the episcopal college also enjoys the same "infallibility in the Magisterium", provided that the bishops "preserve the bond of communion among themselves and with the successor of Peter".

So was everything restored to order with Vatican II?

"In the documents, yes; but not in practice, where another of the paradoxical effects of the post-conciliar period has come to light", he answers. He explains: "The decisive new emphasis on the role of the bishops is in reality restrained or actually risks being smothered by the insertion of bishops into episcopal conferences that are ever more organized, often with burdensome bureaucratic structures. We must not forget that the episcopal conferences have no theological basis, they do not belong to the structure of the Church, as willed by Christ, that cannot be eliminated; they have only a practical, concrete function."

It is, moreover, he says, what is confirmed in the new
Code of Canon Law, which prescribes the extent of the authority of the conferences, which cannot validly act "in the
name of all the bishops unless each and every bishop has
given his consent", unless it concerns "cases in which the
common law prescribes it or a special mandate of the Apostolic See . . . determines it" (CIC, Can. 455, 4 and 1). The
collective, therefore, does not substitute for the persons of
the bishops, who—recalls the Code, confirming the Council—are "the authentic teachers and instructors of the faith
for the faithful entrusted to their care" (cf. CIC Can. 753).
Ratzinger confirms: "No episcopal conference, as such, has
a teaching mission; its documents have no weight of their
own save that of the consent given to them by the individual bishops."

Why does the Prefect insist upon this point? "Because",
he replies, "it is a matter of safeguarding the very nature of
the Catholic Church, which is based on an episcopal structure and not on a kind of federation of national churches.
The national level is not an ecclesial dimension. It must once
again become clear that in each diocese there is only one
shepherd and teacher of the faith in communion with the
other pastors and teachers and with the Vicar of Christ.
The Catholic Church is based on the balance between the
community and the *person*, in this case between the community of individual particular churches united in the universal Church and the *person* of the responsible head of the
diocese."

"It happens", he says, "that with some bishops there is a
certain lack of a sense of individual responsibility, and the
delegation of his inalienable powers as shepherd and teacher
to the structures of the local conference leads to letting what
should remain very personal lapse into anonymity. The group

of bishops united in the conferences depends in their decisions upon other groups, upon commissions that have been established to prepare draft proposals. It happens then that the search for agreement between the different tendencies and the effort at mediation often yield flattened documents in which decisive positions (where they might be necessary) are weakened."

He recalls an episcopal conference that had been held in his country in the thirties: "Well, the really powerful documents against National Socialism were those that came from individual courageous bishops. The documents of the conference, on the contrary, were often rather wan and too weak with respect to what the tragedy called for."

"To find personal courage again"

There is a clear sociological law which—like it or not—guides the workings of groups that are "democratic" only in appearance. This same law (as someone has remarked) operated also in the Council, where in a test session, the second, which took place in 1963, a total of 2135 bishops on the average participated in the meetings in the Aula. Of these only a little more than 200, 10 percent, intervened actively by taking the floor in the debate. The other 90 percent never spoke and limited themselves to listening and to voting.

"Besides," he said, "it is obvious that truth cannot be created through ballots. A statement is either true or false. Truth can only be found, not created. Contrary to a widespread conception, the classic procedure of ecumenical councils did not deviate from this fundamental rule. At these councils only statements that were accepted with a moral unanimity could become binding. This does not at all mean that these unanimously accepted conclusions, at least, could produce truth. If anything, the unanimity of such a large number of bishops of different origins, of different cultural formation and of different temperaments is a sign that they are speaking, not of what they have themselves 'invented', but only of what they have 'found'. Moral unanimity, according to the classic concept of the council, does not possess the character of a vote but that of a testimony.

"If one is clear on this point, there is no further need to demonstrate why an episcopal conference, which moreover represents a much more limited circle than a council, cannot vote on truth. In this regard I should like here to refer to a psychological state of affairs. We Catholic priests of my generation have been habituated to avoiding oppositions among colleagues and to trying always to achieve agreement and not to drawing too much attention to ourselves by taking eccentric positions. Thus, in many episcopal conferences, the group spirit and perhaps even the wish for a quiet, peaceful life or conformism lead the majority to accept the positions of active minorities bent upon pursuing clear goals."

He continues: "I know bishops who privately confess that they would have decided differently than they did at a conference if they had had to decide by themselves. Accepting the group spirit, they shied away from the odium of being viewed as a 'spoilsport', as 'backward', as 'not open'. It seems very nice always to decide *together*. This way, however, entails the risk of losing the 'scandal' and the 'folly' of the Gospel, that 'salt' and that 'leaven' that today are more indispensable than ever for a Christian (above all when he is a bishop, hence invested with precise responsibility for the faithful) in the face of the gravity of the crisis."

In recent years, however, there have been indications of a reverse trend with respect to the first phase of the post-conciliar period: for example, the 1984 plenary assembly of the episcopate of France (it is known that this country often expresses trends of interest to the rest of Catholicism) concentrated on the theme of *recentrage*, of "recentering": a return to the center constituted by Rome, but also a return to that unrelinquishable center that is the diocese, the particular church, her bishop.

It is a trend that is supported, we have heard, by the Congregation for the Doctrine of the Faith, and not only theoretically. In March 1984, the directing staff of the Congregation went to Bogota for the assembly of the doctrinal commissions of the Latin American episcopate. Rome had insisted that the bishops in person and not only their representatives participate in the gathering, "so that the personal responsibility of every individual bishop who, to use the words of the Code, 'is the moderator of the entire ministry of the word', the one upon whom it is incumbent to proclaim the Gospel in the particular church entrusted to him, would be understood (cf. CIC Can. 756,2). This doctrinal responsibility cannot be delegated. On the other hand, there are some who consider even the fact that the bishop personally writes his pastoral letters unacceptable!"

In a document signed by him, Cardinal Ratzinger reminded his brothers in the episcopate of the apostle Paul's serious and passionate exhortation: "Before God and before Christ Jesus who is to be the judge of the living and the dead, I put this duty to you. In the name of his appearing and of his Kingdom: proclaim the message and, welcome or unwelcome, insist on it. . . . Refute falsehood, correct error, call to obedience." The apostle continues (as does Ratzinger's exhortation): "The time is sure to come when, far from being content with sound teaching, people will be avid for the latest novelty and collect for themselves a whole

series of teachers, according to their tastes; and then, instead
of listening to the truth, they will turn to myths. Be careful
always to choose the right course; be brave under trials,
make the preaching of the Good News your life's work, in
thoroughgoing service" (2 Tim 4:1–5).

A disquieting text, I remark, that is suitable to every age.
But for the Prefect, perhaps, it seems to be especially and
strikingly pertinent to our point in time. At any rate what is
expressed therein is the *identity* of the bishop according to
Scripture, as Ratzinger proposes it anew.

Teachers of faith

According to what criterion, I ask him, has Rome in recent
years been guided and inspired in the selection of candidates
for episcopal consecration? Does it still base itself on the
suggestions of the apostolic nuncios, or the "legates of the
pope" (as they are officially called), whom the Holy See has
in every country?

"Yes", he replies. "This task is confirmed by the new
Code: 'It belongs to the pontifical legate to transmit or propose the names of candidates to the Apostolic See in
reference to the naming of bishops and to instruct the infor-
mative process concerning those to be promoted' (CIC Can.
364,4). It is a system which, like all things human, gives rise
to problems, but I wouldn't know how to replace it. There
are countries the vastness of which makes it impossible
for the legate to know all the candidates directly. Hence
episcopal colleges can come into being that are not homoge-
neous. But let us be clear on this particular matter: surely
nobody wants a monotonous, consequently a boring, harmony. Different elements are useful; but it is also necessary

that all be in agreement on fundamental points. The problem is that in the years immediately following the Council, for a certain time, the profile of the ideal 'candidate' was not completely clear."

What do you mean by that?

"In the first years after Vatican II", he explains, "the candidate for the episcopate seemed to be a priest who above all was 'open to the world'. At any rate this criterion came entirely into the foreground. After the turn of 1968 and with the aggravation of the crisis, it was understood that the characteristics associated with this did not alone suffice. Thanks to bitter experiences, it was realized that bishops 'open to the world' were indeed needed but ones who at the same time were capable of opposing the world and its negative tendencies in order to improve them, check them and to warn the faithful against them. The criterion for selection, therefore, gradually became more realistic, the 'opening' as such no longer seemed to suffice as answer and prescription in the altered cultural situations. Besides, a similar maturation took place even with many bishops who had bitterly experienced in their dioceses that the times had really changed with respect to the times of somewhat uncritical optimism after the Council."

The generational change is in progress: at the end of 1984 practically half of the Catholic world episcopate (Joseph Ratzinger included) had not directly participated in Vatican II. Hence a new generation is taking over the guidance of the Church.

A generation that the Prefect would not advise to compete with the professors of theology: "As bishops"—he recently wrote—"their function is not that of also wanting to play an instrument in the concert of specialists." Up-to-date teachers of the faith and zealous shepherds of a flock entrusted to them? Certainly! But their "task rather is to incorporate the voice of the simple faith with its simple and fundamental intuition that precedes science. Faith, indeed, is threatened with destruction every time science sets itself up as an absolute. In this sense, bishops are discharging a function that is altogether *democratic*; a function which, of course, does not depend upon statistics but upon the common gift of baptism."[1]

Rome, despite everything

During one of the pauses in our conversation, I posed a question to him which I meant rather jokingly; the intention was to relax the tension that had been caused by his attempt to make himself understood and by my desire to understand. The answer that he gave, I believe, could in fact help one to understand better his idea of a Church that is based, not on managers, but on men of faith, not on computers, but on love, patience and wisdom.

So I asked him whether he (since he was the former Archbishop of Munich and now a Cardinal in Rome and hence able to make a comparison) would have preferred to have a Church with her center in Germany rather than Italy.

"What a disaster!", he laughed. "We would have an overly organized Church. Just think, in the Munich archbishopric we had 400 staff members and employees, all regularly paid. Now, it is known that because of its nature every office must justify its existence by producing documents, organizing meetings, planning new structures. To be sure, all had the best intentions. But it has often enough happened that the parish priests have felt more burdened than sustained by the quantity of 'auxiliaries'."

[1] *Theologische Prinzipienlehre*, 348.

So Rome, despite everything, is better than rigid structures, the hyper-organization, that fascinate Northern people? "Yes, the Italian spirit is better. With less desire of organizing, it leaves room for those individual personalities, for those singular initiatives, for those original ideas which —as mentioned in connection with the structure of many episcopal conferences—are indispensable for the Church. The saints were all people of imagination, not functionaries of apparatuses. Outwardly, they were perhaps 'unusual' personalities, but nevertheless they were profoundly obedient and, at the same time, persons of great originality and personal independence. And the Church, I shall never tire of repeating it, needs saints more than functionaries. Then I like that Latin humanness that always leaves room for play to the concrete person, even in the necessary network of laws and codices. The law is there for man, and not man for the law: the structure has its justifications, but they must not stifle persons."

The Roman Curia, I say, the controversial reputation that always surrounds it, from the early Middle Ages all through the time of Luther up to our day. . . .

He interrupts me. "I, too, from my native Germany often looked on the Roman apparatus with scepticism, perhaps even with mistrust and impatience. In Rome later I came to realize that this Curia was far superior to its reputation. . . . In the great majority, it is composed of persons who work here in the authentic spirit of service. It cannot be otherwise, considering the modesty of the stipends, which we would consider to be lying on the edge of poverty, and when one also sees that the work of most is a thankless task because it is anonymous and unfolds behind the scenes, preparing documents or positions that will be attributed to others at the summit of the structures."

The accusations of slowness, the proverbial delays in decisions. . . .

He rejoins: "This happens, too, because the Holy See, often suspected of swimming in gold, in reality is not always able to pay for the costs of a more numerous personnel. Many, who think that the 'ex-Holy Office' is an impressive, well-furnished bureau, perhaps cannot imagine that the doctrinal section (perhaps the most important and most attacked by critics of the four sections of which the Congregation is composed) does not number more than about ten persons, the Prefect included. We number about thirty in the whole Congregation. And so a bit less than we would need in order to organize the theological *putsch* which some suspect us of planning! At any rate—joking aside—they are also too few to follow with the necessary punctuality everything afoot in the Church. Not to mention doing justice to that task of 'promotion of the holy doctrine' which the reform places in the first place among our tasks."

How do you manage, then?

"By the establishment of 'faith commissions' in every diocese or episcopal conference. Of course, we preserve the right, by statute, to intervene everywhere in the whole Church. But if it involves events or theories that cause concern, we encourage before all else the bishops or the religious superiors to engage in a dialogue with the author, if they have not already done so. It is only if things are not successfully clarified in this way (or when the problem goes beyond the local borders or assumes international dimensions, or if the local authority itself desires an intervention on the part of Rome) that we engage in a critical dialogue with the author. First of all, we communicate our position to him, elaborated on the basis of an examination of his work, with the opinion of different experts. He has the possibility of correcting us and telling us if we have not rightly interpreted his thought here or there. After an exchange of letters (and sometimes a series of conversations), we answer him, giving him a definitive appraisal and proposing that he present all the clarifications that emerged from the dialogue in an appropriate article."

A procedure, then, that must by itself already require a long time. Don't the lack of personnel and the "Roman" tempo prolong the time, when a timely decision would be called for, often in the interest of the "suspect" who cannot be left in suspense for too long?

"True", he responds, "but I should like to say that the proverbial Vatican slowness does not have negative sides only. This is something else that I first got to understand better in Rome. The art of *soprassedere*, of postponing, as you Italians say, can prove to be positive, can permit the situation to become less tense, to ripen and therefore to clarify itself. Perhaps there is an ancient Latin wisdom here also: overly quick reactions are not always desirable, a swiftness in reflexes that is not so excessive sometimes ends up by respecting persons better."

CHAPTER FIVE

DANGER SIGNS

"An individualistic theology"

As a logical consequence of the crisis of faith in the Church as mystery, where the Gospel lives, entrusted to a hierarchy willed by Christ himself, the Cardinal sees a *crisis of trust in the dogma* proposed by the Magisterium: "Broad circles in theology seem to have forgotten that the subject who pursues theology is not the individual scholar but the Catholic community as a whole, the entire Church. From this forgetfulness of theological work as ecclesial service derives a theological pluralism that in reality is often a subjectivism and individualism that has little to do with the bases of the common tradition. Every theologian now seems to want to be 'creative'. But his proper task is to deepen the common deposit of the faith as well as to help in understanding and proclaiming it, not 'to create' it. Otherwise faith will be fragmentized into a series of often conflicting schools and currents to the grave harm of the disconcerted people of God. In recent years theology has energetically dedicated itself to make faith and signs of the times accord with each other in order to find new ways for the transmission of Christianity. Many, however, have finally come to the realization that these efforts have often contributed more to the aggravation than to the resolution of the crisis. It would be unjust to generalize this affirmation, but it would also be wrong purely and simply to deny it."

Continuing his diagnosis, he says: "In this subjective view of theology, dogma is often viewed as an intolerable strait-jacket, an assault on the freedom of the individual scholar. But this loses sight of the fact that the dogmatic definition is rather a service to the truth, a gift offered to believers by the authority willed by God. Dogmas—someone has said—are not walls that prevent us from seeing. On the contrary, they are windows that open upon the infinite."

"A shattered catechesis"

The confusion that the Prefect notes in theology has, in his opinion, grave consequences for *catechesis*.

He says: "Since theology can no longer transmit a common model of the faith, catechesis is also exposed to dismemberment and to constantly changing experiments. Some catechisms and many catechists no longer teach the Catholic faith in its harmonic wholeness—where each truth presupposes and explains the other—rather they try to make some elements of the Christian patrimony humanly 'interesting' (according to the cultural orientations of the moment). A few biblical passages are set in bold relief because they are viewed as being 'closer to contemporary sensibility'. Others, for the opposite reason, are set aside. Hence it is no longer a catechesis that would constitute a comprehensive, all-embracing formation in the faith, but reflections and flashes of insights deriving from partial, subjective anthropological experiences."

At the beginning of 1983, Ratzinger gave a lecture in France (that caused quite a stir) precisely on the subject of the "new catechesis". On this occasion, with his customary lucidity, he said, among other things: "The first grave error in this direction was to suppress the catechism and to declare quite universally that the category 'catechism' was obsolete." And he speaks of a "hasty and mistaken decision that was most certainly promoted on an international scale."[1]

And to me he repeats: "It must be remembered that from the earliest times of Christianity there appears a permanent and unrelinquishable 'nucleus' of catechesis, hence of formation in the faith. Luther also employed this nucleus for his catechism, in the same matter-of-fact way as did the Roman catechism that had been decided upon at the Council of Trent. All that is said about faith, after all, is organized around four fundamental elements: the *Credo*, the *Our Father*, the *Decalogue*, the *sacraments*. These embrace the foundation of Christian life, the synthesis of the teaching of the Church based on Scripture and tradition. Here the Christian finds all that he must *believe* (the Symbol or Credo), *hope* (the Our Father), *do* (the Decalogue) as well as the *vital space* [*Lebensraum*] in which all this must be accomplished (the sacraments). Today this fundamental structure is neglected in extensive areas of present-day cathechesis. The result, as we note, has been a disintegration of the *sensus fidei* in the new generations, who are often incapable of a comprehensive view of their religion."

At the French conference he told his audience that a mother in Germany had informed him that "her son, a pupil in elementary school, was learning about the christology of the *Logienquelle* but had never yet heard of the seven sacraments or the Apostles' Creed."[2]

---

[1] *Die Krise der Katechese und ihre Überwindung*, 15.
[2] Ibid., 19.

"The broken bond between Church and Scripture"

For Ratzinger the crisis of confidence in the dogma of the Church is accompanied by the contemporary crisis of confidence in the *morality* proposed by the Church. But since, in his view, ethics concerns an area so important that it requires a thorough discussion, we shall report it later. Here we shall first relate his observations on another problem area, namely, the *crisis of confidence in Scripture* as it is read by the Church.

He states: "The bond between Bible and Church has been broken. In the Protestant sphere this separation began at the time of the Enlightenment in the eighteenth century and of late has also found entry into some Catholic scholarly circles. The historico-critical interpretation has certainly opened many and momentous possibilities for a better understanding of the biblical text. But by its very nature, it can illumine it only in its historical dimension and not explain it in its present-day claim on us. Where it forgets this limit it becomes illogical and therefore also unscientific. But then one also forgets that the Bible as present and future can be understood only in a vital association with the Church. The upshot is that one no longer reads it from the tradition of the Church as a point of departure and with the Church, but, instead, one starts from the newest method that presents itself as 'scientific'. With some scholars this independence has become an outright opposition—so much so that for many the traditional faith of the Church no longer seems justified by critical exegesis but appears only as an obstacle to the authentic 'modern' understanding of Christianity."

He will return to this situation in the text when (in asking about the origins) he will consider certain "theologies of liberation".

Here we anticipate his judgment that "the separation of Church and Scripture tends to erode both from within. In fact, a church without a credible biblical foundation is only a chance historical product, one organization among others, and the humanly constructed framework of which we spoke. But the Bible without the Church is also no longer the powerfully effective Word of God, but an assemblage of various historical sources, a collection of heterogeneous books from which one tries to draw, from the perspective of the present moment, whatever one considers useful. An exegesis in which the Bible no longer lives and is understood within the living organism of the Church becomes archaeology: the dead bury their dead. In any case, the last word about the Word of God as Word of God does not in this conception belong to the legitimate pastors, the Magisterium, but to the expert, the professor with his ever-provisional results always subject to revisions."

Consequently, it is necessary for him "that one begin to see the limits of a method that is valuable in itself but that becomes sterile when made absolute. The more one goes beyond the mere observation of past data and strives for a real understanding, the more do philosophical ideas enter which only apparently are a product of the scholarly examination of the text. It can go to such extremes as the absurd experimentations with a 'materialistic interpretation' of the Bible. However today, praise God, among the exegetes themselves an intensive discussion is in progress on the limits of the historico-critical and other modern exegetical methods."

"Through historico-critical research", he continues, "Scripture has again become an *open* book, but also a *closed* one. An *open* book: thanks to the work of exegesis, we perceive the word of the Bible in a new way, in its historical originality, in the manifoldness of the becoming and the growth of a history, laden with tensions and contrast which, at the same time, constitute its unexpected richness. But, in this way, Scripture has again become a *closed* book. It has become the object of experts. The layman, but also the specialist in theology who is not an exegete, can no longer hazard to talk about it. It seems to have almost been withdrawn from the reading and the reflection of the believer, for what would result from this would be dismissed as 'dilettantish'. The science of the specialists has erected a fence around the garden of Scripture to which the nonexpert now no longer has entry."

I ask: Can, then, a "modern" Catholic again begin to read his Bible without bothering himself too much over complicated exegetical questions?

"Certainly", he replies. "Every Catholic must have the courage to believe that his faith (in communion with that of the Church) surpasses every 'new magisterium' of the experts, of the intellectuals. Their hypotheses can be helpful in providing a better understanding of the genesis of the biblical books, but it is a prejudice of evolutionistic provenance if it is asserted that the text is understandable only if its origin and development are studied. The rule of faith, yesterday as today, is not based on the discoveries (be they true or hypothetical) of biblical sources and layers but on the Bible *just as it is*, as it has been read in the Church since the time of the Fathers until now. It is precisely the fidelity to this reading of the Bible that has given us the saints, who were often uneducated and, at any rate, frequently knew nothing about exegetical contexts. Yet they were the ones who understood it best."

"The Son reduced, the Father forgotten"

For him it is obvious that from this spectrum of crises there also derives a crisis that concerns the very foundations: *faith in the triune God* in his Persons. Whereas the theme of the "Holy Spirit" will be treated separately, we shall reproduce here his statements with respect to God the Father and his Son Jesus Christ.

"On the basis of the fear (groundless naturally)", he declares, "that emphasis on the Creator Father could place the Son in the shade, a certain theology today tends to end up completely in christology. But here it is often a matter of a dubious christology, where the human nature of Jesus is unilaterally stressed and the divine, which is united in the same person of Christ, is obscured, passed over in silence or insufficiently expressed. It could be viewed as a return to the realm of the old Arian heresy. Naturally, it would be hard to find a 'Catholic' theologian who states that he would deny the old formula that confesses Jesus as 'Son of God'. All will declare that they accept it, while at the same time instantly adding 'in what sense' that formula is to be understood, in their opinion. And it is precisely here that distinctions operate that often lead to diminishing the faith in Christ as God. As I have already said, christology itself, if it is separated from an ecclesiology that is supernatural and not merely sociological, tends to lose the dimension of the divine, tends to end up in the 'project Jesus', hence in a project of salvation that is merely historical, human."

"As regards the Father, the first Person of the Trinity", he continues, "the 'crisis' concerning him with certain theologians is to be explained on the basis of a society which after Freud mistrusts every father and all fatherhood. The idea of God the Creator is also obscured because the idea of a God whom one must approach on one's knees is not acceptable: one prefers to speak only of partnership, of a relation of friendship, almost among equals, as man to man, with the man Jesus. Then one tends to set aside the question of God the Creator. This happens, too, because one fears the problems (and accordingly would like to avoid them) posed by the relationship between faith in creation and the natural sciences, beginning with the perspectives that have been opened by evolutionism. Thus there are new texts for catechesis which do not begin with Adam, with the beginning of the book of Genesis, but, rather, with the vocation of Abraham or with Exodus. Attention is wholly concentrated on *history*, thus avoiding a confrontation with Being. By so doing, however, God is no longer God—if reduced in this way to Christ alone, if possible even only to the man Jesus. It seems as if de facto a certain theology no longer believes in a God who can enter into the depth of matter. It is like a return to indifference when it is not the gnostic horror of matter. From here arise the doubts on the 'material' aspects of Revelation as well as of the real presence of Christ in the Eucharist, the virginity of Mary, the concrete and real Resurrection of Jesus, the resurrection of the body promised to all at the end of history. It is certainly not accidental that the Apostles' Creed begins with the confession: 'I believe in God, the Father Almighty, Creator of heaven and earth'. This primordial faith in the Creator God (a God who is really God) forms the pivot, as it were, about which all the other Christian truths turn. If vacillation sets in here, all the rest comes tumbling down."

"Restore a place to original sin"

To return to christology: there are those who say that difficulties have arisen also because that reality which theology has called "original sin" is forgotten or denied. Indeed some theologians have made their own the schema of an enlightenment à la Rousseau, with the dogma that lies at the base of modern culture—capitalist or marxist—that of the man good by nature who is corrupted only by false education and by social structures in need of reform. If one wants to change the "system", everything must be properly ordered, and man could then live in peace with himself and with others.

His reply: "If Providence will some day free me of my obligations, I should like to devote myself precisely to the theme of 'original sin' and to the necessity of a rediscovery of its authentic reality. In fact, if it is no longer understood that man is in a state of alienation (that is not only economic and social and, consequently, one that is not resolvable by his efforts alone), one no longer understands the necessity of Christ the Redeemer. The whole structure of the faith is threatened by this. The inability to understand 'original sin' and to make it understandable is really one of the most difficult problems of present-day theology and pastoral ministry."

But perhaps it is necessary, I interject, to reflect on the linguistic level also: is the old expression "original sin", which is of patristic origin, still adequate today?

"It's always very dangerous to change religious language. Continuity here is of great importance. I hold that the central concepts of the faith, which derive from the great utterances of Scripture, cannot be altered: as, for example, 'Son of God', 'Holy Spirit', Mary's 'virginity' and 'divine motherhood'. I grant, however, that expressions such as 'original sin', which in their content are also directly biblical in origin but which already manifest in expression the stage of theological reflection, are modifiable. At all events, one must proceed with great care: the words are not unimportant; rather they are closely bound to the meaning. I believe, nevertheless, that the theological and pastoral difficulties in the face of 'original sin' are certainly not only of a semantic but also of a deeper nature."

What does that mean in particular?

"In an evolutionist hypothesis of the world (which corresponds to a certain 'Teilhardism' in theology), there is obviously no place for an 'original sin'. This, at most, is merely a symbolic, mythical expression to designate the *natural* deficiencies of a creature like man, who, from most imperfect origins, moves toward perfection, toward his complete realization. Acceptance of this view signifies, however, turning the structure of Christianity on its head: Christ is displaced from the past to the future. Salvation would simply mean moving toward the future as the necessary development to the better. Man is but a product who has not yet been fully perfected by time. There has never been a 'redemption' because there was no sin on account of which man would need to be healed, but only, I repeat, a natural deficiency. Yet these difficulties of more or less 'scientific' origin are not yet the root of the present-day crisis of 'original sin'. This crisis is only a symptom of our profound difficulty in perceiving the reality of our own selves, of the world and of God. Discussions with the natural sciences, with for example paleontology, certainly do not suffice, even though this kind of confrontation is necessary. We must be aware that we, too, are in the presence of prior understandings and prior decisions of a philosophic character."

At any rate, they are understandable difficulties, I remark, given the really "mysterious" character of "original sin", or whatever one may wish to call it.

He says: "This Christian truth is, on the one hand, a mystery; but on the other, it is also, in a way, evident. What is *evident*: a lucid, realistic view of man and of history cannot but stumble upon their alienation and discover that there is a rupture in relationships: in man's relationship to himself, to others, to God. Now, since man is preeminently a being-in-relationship, such a rupture reaches to the very roots and affects all else. The *mystery*: if we are not able to penetrate to the depths the reality and the consequences of original sin, it is precisely because it exists, because the derangement is ontological, because it unbalances, confuses in us the logic of nature, thus preventing us from understanding how a fault at the origin of history can draw in its wake a situation of common sin."

Adam, Eve, Eden, the apple, the serpent. . . . What should we think of them?

"The biblical narrative of the origins does not relate events in the sense of modern historiography, but rather, it speaks through images. It is a narrative that *reveals* and *hides* at the same time. But the underpinning elements are reasonable, and the reality of the dogma must at all events be safeguarded. The Christian would be remiss toward his brethren if he did not proclaim the Christ who first and foremost brings redemption from sin; if he did not proclaim the reality of the alienation (the 'Fall') and, at the same time, the reality of the grace that redeems us, that liberates us; if he did not proclaim that, in order to effect a restoration of our original nature, a help from outside is necessary; if he did not proclaim that the insistence upon self-realization, upon self-salvation does not lead to redemption but to destruction; finally, if he did not proclaim that, in order to be saved, it is necessary to abandon oneself to Love."

CHAPTER SIX

THE DRAMA OF MORALITY

From liberalism to permissivism

So there is also a *crisis* — likewise grave — *of the morality* proposed by the Magisterium of the Church. A crisis, as we have already said, closely linked to that affecting Catholic dogma.

It is a crisis that for the moment affects the so-called "developed" world, particularly Europe and the United States. But, as we know, the models elaborated in these zones eventually end up in the rest of the world with the help of a well-known cultural imperialism.

At any rate, to quote the Cardinal, "In a world like the West, where money and wealth are the measure of all things, and where the model of the free market imposes its implacable laws on every aspect of life, authentic Catholic ethics now appears to many like an alien body from times long past, as a kind of meteorite which is in opposition, not only to the concrete habits of life, but also to the way of thinking underlying them. Economic *liberalism* creates its exact counterpart, *permissivism*, on the moral plane." Accordingly, "it becomes difficult, if not altogether impossible, to present Catholic morality as reasonable. It is too distant from what is considered to be obvious, as normal by the majority of persons, conditioned by the dominant culture with which not a few 'Catholic' moralists have aligned themselves as influential supporters."

In Bogota, at the meeting of the bishops who preside over the doctrinal commissions and episcopal conferences of Latin America, the Cardinal read a report — unpublished up to now — that tried to single out the deep motives of what was transpiring in contemporary theology, including moral theology, which was allotted a space corresponding to its importance in that report. Hence it will be necessary to follow Ratzinger in his analysis in order to understand his alarm in the face of certain paths upon which the West, and in its suite, certain theologies, have entered. He intends above all to draw attention to questions of family and sexuality.

"A series of ruptures"

Accordingly he observes: "In the culture of the 'developed' world it is above all the indissoluble bond between *sexuality* and *motherhood* that has been ruptured. Separated from motherhood, sex has remained without a locus and has lost its point of reference: it is a kind of drifting mine, a problem and at the same time an omnipresent power."

After this first rupture he sees another, as a consequence: "After the separation between sexuality and motherhood was effected, sexuality was also separated from procreation. The movement, however, ended up going in an opposite direction: procreation without sexuality. Out of this follow the increasingly shocking medical-technical experiments so prevalent in our day where, precisely, procreation is independent of sexuality. Biological manipulation is striving to uncouple man from nature (the very existence of which is being disputed). There is an attempt to transform man, to manipulate him as one does every other 'thing': he is nothing but a product planned according to one's pleasure."

If I am not mistaken, I observe, our cultures are the first in history in which such ruptures have come to pass.

"Yes, and at the end of this march to shatter fundamental, natural linkages (and not, as is said, only those that are cultural), there are unimaginable consequences which, however, derive from the very logic that lies at the base of a venture of this kind."

In his view we will atone already in our day for "the consequences of a sexuality which is no longer linked to motherhood and to procreation. It logically follows from this that every form of sexuality is equivalent and therefore of equal worth." "It is certainly not a matter", he specifies, "of establishing or recommending a retrograde moralism, but one of lucidly drawing the consequences from the premises: it is, in fact, logical that pleasure, the *libido* of the individual, become the only possible point of reference of sex. No longer having an objective reason to justify it, sex seeks the subjective reason in the gratification of the desire, in the most 'satisfying' answer for the individual, to the instincts no longer subject to rational restraints. Everyone is free to give to his personal *libido* the content considered suitable for himself."

He continues: "Hence, it naturally follows that all forms of sexual gratification are transformed into the 'rights' of the individual. Thus, to cite an especially current example, homosexuality becomes an inalienable right. (Given the aforementioned premises, how can one deny it?) On the contrary, its full recognition appears to be an aspect of human liberation."

There are, however, other consequences of "this uprooting of the human person in the depth of his nature". He elaborates: "Fecundity separated from marriage based on a lifelong fidelity turns from being a *blessing* (as it was understood in every culture) into its opposite: that is to say a *threat* to the free development of the 'individual's right to happiness'. Thus abortion, institutionalized, free and socially guaranteed, becomes another 'right', another form of 'liberation'."

"Far from society or far from the Magisterium?"

This, then, is how the dramatic ethical scenario of the liberal–radical "affluent" society presents itself to him. But how does Catholic moral theology react to all this?

"The now dominant mentality attacks the very foundations of the morality of the Church, which, as I have already said, if she remains true to herself, risks appearing like an anachronistic construct, a bothersome, alien body. Thus the moral theologians of the Western Hemisphere, in their efforts to still remain 'credible' in our society, find themselves facing a difficult alternative: it seems to them that they must choose between opposing modern society and opposing the Magisterium. The number of those who prefer the latter type of opposition is larger or smaller depending on how the question is posed: consequently they set out on a search for theories and systems that allow compromises between Catholicism and current conceptions. But this growing difference between the Magisterium and the 'new' moral theologies leads to unforeseeable consequences, also precisely for the reason that the Church with her schools and her hospitals still occupies an important social role (especially in America). Thus we stand before the difficult alternative: either the Church finds an understanding, a compromise with the values propounded by society which she wants to continue to serve, or she decides to remain faithful to her own values (and in the Church's view these are the values that protect man in his deepest needs) as the result of which she finds herself on the margin of society."

Thus the Cardinal believes he can observe that "today the sphere of moral theology has become the main locus of the tensions between Magisterium and theologians, especially because here the consequences are most immediately perceptible. I should like to cite some trends: at times premarital relations, at least under certain conditions, are justified. Masturbation is presented as a normal phenomenon of adolescence. Admission of remarried divorced couples to the sacraments is constantly demanded. Radical feminism—especially in some women's religious orders—also seems to be gaining ground noticeably in the Church (but we will speak about that later). Even as regards the question of homosexuality, attempts at its justification are in the making. Indeed, it has come to pass that bishops—on the basis of insufficient information or also because of a sense of guilt among Catholics toward an 'oppressed minority'—have placed churches at the disposal of '*gays*' for their gatherings. Then there is the case of *Humanae vitae*, the encyclical of Paul VI, which reaffirmed the 'no' to contraceptives and which has not been understood. Instead it has been more or less openly rejected in broad ecclesial circles "

But, I ask, is it not precisely the problem of birth control that finds traditional Catholic morality rather helpless? Doesn't one get the impression that here the Magisterium has exposed itself by its lack of solid, decisive arguments?

"It's true", he replies, "that at the beginning of the great debate following the appearance of the encyclical *Humanae vitae* in 1968, the demonstrative basis of the theology faithful to the Magisterium was still relatively slim. But, in the meantime, it has been broadened through new experiences and new reflections so that the situation is beginning to reverse itself. In order to understand the whole problem correctly, we are here obliged to take a look at the past. In the thirties or forties, some Catholic moral theologians had begun to criticize the onesidedness of the orientation of Catholic sexual morality toward procreation from the point of view of personalist philosophy. Above all they called attention to the fact that the classic treatment of marriage in Canon law, based on its 'ends', did not do full justice to the essence of marriage. The category 'end' is insufficient to explain this peculiarly human phenomenon. In no way did these theologians deny the importance of fecundity in the complex of values of human sexuality. But they assigned a new place to it within the framework of a more personalistic perspective in the way of considering marriage. These discussions were important and have produced a significant deepening of the Catholic doctrine on matrimony. The Council accepted and confirmed the best aspects of these reflections. But at this point in time a new line of development began to materialize. Whereas the reflections of the Council were based on the unity of person and nature in man, personalism began to be understood in opposition to 'naturalism' (as if the human person and its needs could enter into conflict with nature). Thus an exaggerated personalism led some theologians to reject the internal order, the language of nature (which instead is moral of itself, according to the constant teaching of the Catholic Church), leaving to sexuality, conjugal included, the sole point of reference in the will of the person. This indeed is one of the reasons that *Humanae vitae* was rejected and that it is impossible for many theologies to reject contraception."

Seeking fixed points of reference

In his view, "exaggerated personalism" is not the only ethical system being developed as an alternative to those of the Magisterium. Ratzinger—referring to the moral-theological discussions in the Western world—delineated to the bishops assembled in Bogota the lines of other systems that he considers unacceptable: "Immediately after the Council, discussions were begun as to whether specifically Christian moral norms, as such, existed. Some came to the conclusion that all the norms can also be found outside the Christian world and that, de facto, the greater part of Christian norms came from other cultures, particularly from ancient classic culture, especially the stoic. From this erroneous point of departure, they arrived unavoidably at the idea that morality was to be constructed solely on the basis of reason and that this autonomy of reason was also valid for believers. Hence no more Magisterium, no more God of Revelation with his Decalogue. In fact, many espoused the view that the Decalogue on which the Church has based her objective morality is nothing but a 'cultural product' linked to the ancient Semitic Middle East. Hence a relative norm dependent on an anthropology and on a history that is no longer ours. And so here we again find the denial of the unity of Scripture, the resurfacing of the old heresy which held that the Old Testament (the locus of the 'law') was surpassed and replaced by the New (kingdom of 'grace'). But for Catholics, the Bible is a unitary whole; the beatitudes of Jesus do not annul the Decalogue, which had been given by God to Moses and through him to men of all times. Instead, according to these new moral theologians, since we are 'now adult and liberated', we ought to seek other behavioral norms by ourselves."[1]

[1] Unpublished address in Bogota.

A search, I say, to be conducted on the basis of reason alone?

"As I have already indicated," he replied, "it is known that in the final analysis for genuine Catholic morality there are actions that reason will never be able to justify, since they contain in themselves rejection of the Creator God and therefore a denial of the authentic good of man, his creature. For the Magisterium there have always been fixed points of reference, landmarks which can neither be removed nor ignored without breaking the bond that Christian philosophy sees between *Being* and the *Good*. By proclaiming, instead, the autonomy of human reason alone, now detached from the Decalogue, one is forced to embark on a search for new fixed points: to what shall one adhere, how are moral duties to be justified if they are no longer rooted in divine Revelation, in the commandments of the Creator?"

What then?

"Well, one has arrived at the so-called 'morality of ends' — or, as it is preferred in the United States where it is particularly developed and diffused — of 'consequences', '*consequentialism*': Nothing *in itself* is good or bad, the goodness of an act depends entirely upon its end and upon its foreseeable and calculated consequences. After becoming aware of the problematic character of such a system, some moralists have attempted to tone down 'consequentialism' to '*proportionalism*': moral conduct depends upon the evaluation and weighing of the proportion of goods that are involved. Again it is a matter of individual evaluation, this time an evaluation of the 'proportion' between good and evil."

It seems to me, however, I observe, that the classical morality also made reference to calculations of such a kind: the evaluation of the consequences, the weighing of the goods involved.

"Of course", he replies. "The error lies in constructing a system on what was only an aspect of the traditional morality which certainly — in the final analysis — did not depend upon the personal evaluation of the individual, but upon the Revelation of God, upon the 'instructions for use' inscribed by him objectively and indelibly in his creation. Accordingly, nature, and with it precisely also man himself, so far as he is part of that created nature, contain that morality within themselves."

In the Prefect's view, the negation of all this leads to shattering consequences for the individual and for the entire society: "If we turn from the affluent societies of the West, where these systems cropped up for the first time, we find that in the moral convictions of many liberation theologies, a 'proportionalist' morality also often stands in the background. The 'absolute good' (and this means the building of a just socialist society) becomes the moral norm that justifies everything else, including — if necessary — violence, homicide, mendacity. It is one of the many aspects that show how mankind, when it loses its mooring in God, falls prey to the most arbitrary consequences. The 'reason' of the individual, in fact, can from case to case propose the most different, the most unforeseeable and the most dangerous ends. And what looks like 'liberation' turns into its opposite and shows its diabolic visage in deeds. Actually, all this has already been described with precision in the first pages of the Bible. The core of the temptation for man and of his fall is contained in this programmatic statement: 'You will be like God' (Gen 3:5). Like God: that means free of the law of the Creator, free of the laws of nature herself, absolute lord of one's own destiny. Man continually desires only one thing: to be his own creator and his own master. But what awaits us at the end of this road is certainly not Paradise."

CHAPTER SEVEN

WOMEN, A WOMAN

A priesthood in question

For the Cardinal the problem-complex of the crisis of morality is closely tied to that (extremely topical in the Church today) of woman and her role.

The document of the Congregation for the Doctrine of the Faith that repeated the Catholic "no" (shared by all the Eastern Orthodox churches and until recently also by the Anglicans) to feminine priesthood bears the signature of Cardinal Ratzinger's predecessor. Ratzinger, however, contributed to it as a consultant, and, in reply to my question, he was to define it as "very well prepared even though, like all official documents, it is marked by a certain dryness: it goes directly to the conclusions without being able to justify all the individual steps leading to them with the requisite fullness of detail."

It is that document, however, to which the Prefect refers in order to pursue a question that, in his view, is often wrongly formulated. When speaking of the women's question in general (and of its repercussions on the Church and in particular among women religious), there is the ring of a certain sadness in his words: "It is precisely woman who most harshly suffers the consequences of the confusion, of the superficiality of a culture that is the fruit of masculine attitudes of mind, masculine ideologies, which deceive woman, uproot her in the depths of her being, while claiming that in reality they want to liberate her."

Therefore he states: "At first sight it seems that the demands of radical feminism in favor of a total equality between man and woman are extremely noble and, at any rate, perfectly reasonable. It also seems logical that the demand that women be allowed to enter all professions, excluding none, should transform itself within the Church into a demand for access also to the priesthood. To many, this demand for the ordination of women, this possibility of having Catholic priestesses, appears not only justified but obvious: a simple and inevitable adaptation of the Church to a new social situation that has come into being."

In that case, I ask, why does one persist in refusing the demand?

"In reality", he replies, "this kind of 'emancipation' of woman is in no way new. One forgets that in the ancient world all the religions also had priestesses. All except one: the Jewish. Christianity, here too following the 'scandalous' original example of Jesus, opens a new situation to women; it accords them a position that represents a novelty with respect to Judaism. But of the latter he preserves the exclusively male priesthood. Evidently, Christian intuition understood that the question was not secondary, that to defend Scripture (which in neither the Old nor the New Testament knows women priests) signified once more to defend the human person, especially those of the female sex."

Against "trivialized" sex

The matter requires, I remark, a further clarification: it still remains to be seen in what way the Bible and the tradition

that has interpreted it attribute "equality" to women and at
the same time exclude her from the priesthood.

"Certainly," he concedes, "but it is further necessary to
get to the bottom of the demand that radical feminism
draws from the widespread modern culture, namely, the
'trivialization' of sexual specificity that makes every role interchangeable between man and woman. When we were
speaking of the crisis of traditional morality, I indicated a
series of fatal ruptures: that, for example, between sexuality
and procreation. Detached from the bond with fecundity,
sex no longer appears to be a determined characteristic, as a
radical and pristine orientation of the person. Male? Female?
They are questions that for some are now viewed as obsolete,
senseless, if not racist. The answer of current conformism is
foreseeable: 'whether one is male or female has little interest
for us, we are all simply humans'. This, in reality, has grave
consequences even if at first it appears very beautiful and
generous. It signifies, in fact, that sexuality is no longer
rooted in anthropology; it means that sex is viewed as a simple role, interchangeable at one's pleasure."

What follows from that?

"What follows with logical necessity is that the whole
being and the whole activity of the human person are reduced to pure functionality, to the pure role: depending on
the social context, for example, to the role of 'consumer' or
the role of 'worker'; at any rate to something that does not
directly regard the respective sex. It is not by chance that
among the battles of 'liberation' of our time there has also
been that of escaping from the 'slavery of nature', demanding the right to be male or female at one's will or pleasure,
for example, through surgery, and demanding that the State
record this autonomous will of the individual in its registry
offices. Incidentally, one must realize that this so-called sex

change alters nothing in the genetic constitution of the person involved. It is only an external artifact which resolves no problems but only constructs fictitious realities. Nor is it by chance that the laws immediately adapted themselves to such a demand. If everything is only a culturally and historically conditioned 'role', and not a natural specificity inscribed in the depth of being, even motherhood is a mere accidental function. In fact, certain feminist circles consider it 'unjust' that only the woman is forced to give birth and to suckle. And not only the law but science, too, offers a helping hand: by transforming a male into a female and vice-versa, as we have already seen, or by separating fecundity from sexuality with the purpose of making it possible to procreate at will, with the help of technical manipulations. Are we not, after all, all alike? So, if need be one also fights against nature's 'inequity'. But one cannot struggle against nature without undergoing the most devastating consequences. The sacrosanct equality between man and woman does not exclude, indeed it requires, diversity."

In defense of nature

From a general discussion of the problem-complex, let us pass on to what interests us most. What happens when these trends of thought gain entry into the religious, Christian sphere?

"What happens is that the interchangeableness of the sexes, viewed as simple 'roles' determined more by history than by nature, and the trivialization of male and female extend to the very idea of God and from there spread out to the whole religious reality."

Yet, it seems that even a Catholic can maintain (indeed, a

Pope has recently recalled it) that God is beyond the categories of his creation. Hence he is Mother as well as Father.

"This is in fact correct", he replies, "insofar as we place ourselves on a purely philosophic, abstract point of view. But Christianity is not a philosophical speculation; it is not a construction of our mind. Christianity is not 'our' work; it is a *Revelation*; it is a message that has been consigned to us, and we have no right to reconstruct it as we like or choose. Consequently, we are not authorized to change the *Our Father* into an *Our Mother*: the symbolism employed by Jesus is irreversible; it is based on the same Man-God relationship that he came to reveal to us. Even less is it permissible to replace Christ with another figure. But what radical feminism — at times even that which asserts that it is based on Christianity — is not prepared to accept is precisely this: the exemplary, universal, unchangeable relationship between Christ and the Father."

If these are the positions confronting one another, I remark, dialogue seems impossible.

"I am, in fact, convinced", he says "that what feminism promotes in its radical form is no longer the Christianity that we know; it is another religion. But I am also convinced (we are beginning to see the deep reasons of the biblical position) that the Catholic Church and the Eastern Churches will defend their faith and their concept of the priesthood, thereby defending in reality both men and women in their totality as well as in their irreversible differentiation into male and female, hence in their irreducibility to simple function or role."

"Besides," he continues, "what I shall never tire of repeating also applies here: for the Church the *language of nature* (in our case, two sexes complementary to each other yet quite distinct) is *also the language of morality* (man and woman called to equally noble destinies, both eternal, but different). It is precisely in the name of nature—it is known that Protestant tradition and, in its wake, that of the Enlightenment mistrust this concept—that the Church raises her voice against the temptation to project persons and their destiny according to mere human plans, to strip them of individuality and, in consequence, of dignity. To respect biology is to respect God himself, hence to safeguard his creatures."

According to Ratzinger, this, too, is the fruit "of the opulent West and of its intellectual *establishment*." Feminine radicalism "announces a liberation that is a salvation different from, if not opposed to, the Christian conception." But, he warns: "The men and above all the women who are experiencing the fruits of this presumed post-Christian salvation must realistically ask themselves if this really signifies an increase of happiness, a greater balance, a vital synthesis, richer than the one discarded because it was deemed to be obsolete."

So, I ask, in your opinion, appearances would be deceiving? Rather than being beneficiaries, women are victims of the "revolution" in progress?

"Yes," he replies, "it is precisely woman who is paying the greatest price. Motherhood and virginity (the two loftiest values in which she realizes her profoundest vocation) have become values that are in opposition to the dominant ones. Woman, who is creative in the truest sense of the word by giving life, does not 'produce', however, in that technical sense which is the only one that is valued by a society more masculine than ever in its cult of efficiency. She is being convinced that the aim is to 'liberate' her, 'emancipate' her, by encouraging her to masculinize herself, thus bringing her into conformity with the culture of production and subjecting her to the control of the masculine society of technicians, of salesmen, of politicians who seek profit and power, organizing everything, marketing everything, instrumentalizing everything for their own ends. While asserting that sexual differentiation is in reality secondary (and, accordingly, denying the body itself as an incarnation of the spirit in a sexual being), woman is robbed not only of motherhood but also of the free choice of virginity. Yet, just as man cannot procreate without her, likewise he cannot be virgin save by 'imitating' woman who, also in this way, has a surpassing value as 'sign', as 'example' for the other part of humanity."

Feminism in the convent

How do things stand, I ask, in that manifold and complex world (often impenetrable to a man, especially if he is a layman), namely, the world of women religious: sisters, nuns and all the others who have consecrated themselves to God?

"A feminist mentality", he replies, "has also entered into women's religious orders. This is particularly evident, even in its most extreme forms, on the North American continent. On the other hand, the cloistered contemplative orders have withstood very well because they are more sheltered from the *Zeitgeist*, and because they are characterized by a clear and unalterable aim: praise of God, prayer, virginity and separation from the world as an eschatological sign. On the other hand, active orders and congregations are in grave crisis: the discovery of professionalism, the concept of 'social welfare' which has replaced that of 'love of neighbor', the often uncritical and yet enthusiastic adaptation to the new and hitherto unknown values of modern secular

society, the entrance into the convents, at times wholly
unexamined, of psychologies and psychoanalyses of different
tendencies: all this has led to the burning problems of identity
and, with many women, to the collapse of motivations sufficient to justify religious life. Visiting a Catholic bookshop in
Latin America, I noticed that there (and not only there) the
spiritual treatises of the past had been replaced by the
widespread manuals of psychoanalysis. Theology had made
way for psychology, where possible to the one most in
vogue. Almost irresistible, moreover, was the fascination for
what is Eastern or presumed such: in many religious houses
(of both men and women) the cross has at times given up its
place to symbols of the Asiatic religious tradition. In some
places the previous devotions have also disappeared in order
to make way for yoga or Zen techniques."

It has been observed, and we have have already spoken
about it, that many men religious have tried to solve the
identity crisis by shifting *to the exterior*, according to the
well-known masculine dynamic, thus seeking "liberation"
in society, in politics. Many women religious, instead, seem
to have shifted *to the interior* (following here too a dialectic
linked to sex), pursuing that same "liberation" in depth
psychology.

"Yes," he says, "some have turned with great trust to
these profane confessors, to these 'experts of the soul' that
psychologists and psychoanalysts supposedly are. But these
can say at most *how* the forces of the mind function, they
cannot say *why, to what purpose*. Now, the crisis of many
Sisters, of many women religious, was determined precisely
by the circumstance that their mind seemed to be working
in a void, without a discernible direction any more. Precisely through these incessant analyses it has been made very
clear that the 'soul' does not explain itself by itself, that it

needs a point of reference outside itself. It was almost a 'scientific' confirmation of St. Augustine's passionate perception, 'Thou hast made us for thyself, O Lord, and our heart is restless until it rests in thee'. This searching and experimenting, often entrusting oneself to self-styled 'experts', has led to unforeseeable human burdens, at any rate to very great ones for women religious, for those who have remained as well as for those who have left."

A future without Sisters?

There is a recent and detailed report on the women religious of Quebec, the French-speaking province of Canada. Quebec is an exemplary case: in fact it was the only region in North America which from the very outset was colonized and evangelized by Catholics who established a Christian regime there, administered by an omnipresent Church. In fact, up to twenty years ago at the beginning of the sixties, Quebec was the region of the world with the highest number of women religious in relation to the population, which totaled six million. Between 1961 and 1981, the women religious, as the result of departures, deaths, decline in recruitment, have been reduced from 46,933 to 26,294. Hence a drop of 44 percent with no end in sight. New vocations, in fact, declined 98.5 percent in the same period. It turns out, furthermore, that the greater part of the remaining 1.5 percent does not consist of young people but of "late vocations", so that, on the basis of a simple projection, all sociologists agree in a gloomy but objective prognosis: "Soon (unless there is a reversal of the trend, which is wholly improbable, at least viewed humanly) women's religious life as we have known it will be only a memory in Canada."

The same sociologists who prepared the report describe how, in these twenty years, all the communities had begun every kind of reform imaginable: abandonment of the religious habit, individual stipends, degrees in secular universities, insertion into secular professions, a massive assistance by every type of "specialist". Nevertheless, the Sisters continued to leave, new ones did not arrive, those who remained—the average age is about sixty—often do not seem to have resolved the identity problem, and in some cases many say they are resignedly awaiting the extinction of their congregations.

The *aggiornamento*, even the most courageous, was necessary. But it seems not to have functioned properly, especially in North America, to which Ratzinger specifically refers here. Was it perhaps because, by forgetting the evangelical admonition, an attempt was made to pour *"new wine"* into *"old wine-skins"*, that is, into communities born in another spiritual climate, thus children of a *societas christiana* that is no longer ours? And so consequently, the end of *a* religious life does not necessarily mean the end of *the* religious life, which will incarnate itself in new forms, adapted to our times?

The Prefect certainly does not exclude this, even though the Quebec example confirms that the orders apparently most opposed to the modern mentality and least receptive to change, the cloistered contemplative ones, "have at most registered some problems but have not experienced a real crisis", if we go along with the words of the sociologists themselves.

Be that as it may, for the Cardinal, "if it is woman who must pay the highest price to the new society and its values, among all women the Sisters were the most affected." Returning to what had already been pointed out, he remarks:

"The man, even the religious, despite the well-known problems, was able to make his way out of the crisis by throwing
himself into work whereby he tried to discover his role
anew in activity. But what is the woman to do when the
roles inscribed in her own biology have been denied and perhaps even ridiculed? If her wonderful capacity to give love,
help, solace, warmth, solidarity has been replaced by the
economistic and trade-union mentality of the 'profession',
by this typical masculine concern? What can the woman do
when all that is most particularly hers is swept away and
declared irrelevant and deviant?"

He continues: "Activism, the will to be 'productive', 'relevant', come what may, is the constant temptation of the
man, even of the male religious. And this is precisely the basic
trend in the ecclesiologies (we spoke about it) that present the
Church as a 'People of God' committed to action, busily
engaged in translating the Gospel into an action program
with social, political and cultural objectives. But it is no accident if the word 'Church' is of feminine gender. In her, in
fact, lives the mystery of motherhood, of gratitude, of contemplation, of beauty, of values in short that appear useless in
the eyes of the profane world. Without perhaps being fully
conscious of the reasons, the woman religious feels the deep
disquiet of living in a Church where Christianity is reduced
to an ideology of doing, according to that strictly masculine
ecclesiology which nevertheless is presented—and perhaps believed—as being closer also to women and their 'modern'
needs. Instead it is the project of a Church in which there is
no longer any room for mystical experience, for this pinnacle
of religious life which not by chance has been, through the
centuries, among the glories and riches offered to all in un-
broken constancy and fullness, more by women than by men.
Those extraordinary women whom the *Church* has proclaimed

her 'saints', and occasionally even her 'doctors', never hesitating to propose them as an example to all Christians. An example that today is perhaps of special relevance."

A remedy: Mary

To the crisis in the understanding of the Church, to the crisis of morality, to the crisis of woman, the Prefect has a remedy, among others, to propose "that has concretely shown its effectiveness throughout the centuries." "A remedy whose reputation seems to be clouded today with some Catholics but one that is more than ever relevant." It is the remedy that he designates with a short name: *Mary*.

Ratzinger is very aware that it is precisely mariology which presents a facet of Christianity to which certain groups regain access only with difficulty, even though it was confirmed by the Second Vatican Council as the culmination of the Dogmatic Constitution on the Church. "By inserting the mystery of Mary into the mystery of the Church", he says, "Vatican II made an important decision which should have given a new impetus to theological research. Instead, in the early post-conciliar period, there has been a sudden decline in this respect — almost a collapse, even though there are now signs of a new vitality."

In 1968, eighteen years after the proclamation of the dogma of the Assumption of Mary in body and soul to heavenly glory, the then professor Ratzinger observed as he recalled the event: "The fundamental orientation which guides our lives in only a few years has so changed that today we find it difficult to understand the enthusiasm and the joy that then reigned in so many parts of the Catholic Church. . . . Since then much has changed, and today that dogma which at that time so uplifted us instead escapes us. We ask ourselves whether with it we may not be placing unnecessary obstacles in the way of a reunion with our evangelical fellow Christians, whether it would not be much easier if this stone did not lie on the road, this stone which we ourselves had placed there in the so recent past. We also ask ourselves whether with such a dogma we may not threaten the orientation of Christian piety. Will it not be misdirected, instead of looking toward God the Father and toward the sole mediator, Jesus Christ, who as man is our brother and at the same time is so one with God that he is himself God?"

Yet, during the interview he told me, "If the place occupied by Mary has been essential to the equilibrium of the Faith, today it is urgent, as in few other epochs of Church history, to rediscover that place."

Ratzinger's testimony is also humanly important, having been arrived at along a personal path of rediscovery, of gradual deepening, almost in the sense of a full "conversion", of the Marian mystery. In fact, he confides to me: "As a young theologian in the time before (and also during) the Council, I had, as many did then and still do today, some reservations in regard to certain ancient formulas, as, for example, that famous *De Maria nunquam satis,* 'concerning Mary one can never say enough.' It seemed exaggerated to me. So it was difficult for me later to understand the true meaning of another famous expression (current in the Church since the first centuries when—after a memorable dispute—the Council of Ephesus, in 431, had proclaimed Mary *Theotokos,* Mother of God). The declaration, namely, that designated the Virgin as *'the conqueror of all heresies'.* Now—in this confused period where truly every type of heretical aberration seems to be pressing upon the doors of the authentic faith—now I understand that it was not a matter of pious exaggerations, but of truths that today are more valid than ever."

"Yes", he continues, "it is necessary to go back to Mary if we want to return to that 'truth about Jesus Christ', 'truth about the Church' and the 'truth about man' that John Paul II proposed as a program to the whole of Christianity when, in 1979, he opened the Latin American episcopal conference in Puebla. The bishops responded to the Pope's proposal by including in the first documents (the very ones that have been read only incompletely by some) their unanimous wish and concern: 'Mary must be more than ever *the pedagogy*, in order to proclaim the Gospel to the men of today.' Precisely in that continent where the traditional Marian piety of the people is in decline, the resultant void is being filled by political ideologies. It is a phenomenon that can be noted almost everywhere to a certain degree, confirming the importance of that piety which is no mere piety."

Six reasons for not forgetting

The Cardinal lists six points in which—albeit in a very concise and therefore necessarily incomplete way—he sees the importance of Mary with regard to the equilibrium and completeness of the Catholic Faith.

First point: "When one recognizes the place assigned to Mary by dogma and tradition, one is solidly rooted in authentic christology. (According to Vatican II: 'Devoutly meditating on her and contemplating her in the light of the Word made man, the Church reverently *penetrates more deeply into the great mystery of the Incarnation* and becomes more and more like her spouse' [*Lumen Gentium*, no. 65].) It is, moreover in direct service to faith in Christ—not, therefore, primarily out of devotion to the Mother—that the Church has proclaimed her Marian dogmas: first that of her perpetual virginity and divine motherhood and then, after a long period of maturation and reflection, those of her Immaculate Conception and bodily Assumption into heavenly glory. These dogmas protect the original faith in Christ as true God and true man: two natures in a single Person. They also secure the indispensable eschatological tension by pointing to Mary's Assumption as the immortal destiny that awaits us all. And they also protect the faith—threatened today—in God the Creator, who (and this, among other things, is the meaning of the truth of the perpetual virginity of Mary, more than ever not understood today) can freely intervene also in matter. Finally, Mary, as the Council recalls: 'having entered deeply into the history of salvation, . . . in a way *unites in her person and reechoes the most important mysteries of the Faith*' (*Lumen Gentium*, no. 65)."

This first point is followed by a *second*: "The mariology of the Church comprises the right relationship, the necessary integration between Scripture and tradition. The *four* Marian dogmas have their clear foundation in sacred Scripture. But it is there like a seed that grows and bears fruit in the life of tradition just as it finds expression in the liturgy, in the perception of the believing people and in the reflection of theology guided by the Magisterium."

Third point: "In her very person as a Jewish girl become the mother of the Messiah, Mary binds together, in a living and indissoluble way, the old and the new People of God, Israel and Christianity, synagogue and church. She is, as it were, the connecting link without which the Faith (as is happening today) runs the risk of losing its balance by either forsaking the New Testament for the Old or dispensing with the Old. In her, instead, we can live the unity of sacred Scripture in its entirety."

Fourth point: "The correct Marian devotion guarantees to faith the coexistence of indispensable 'reason' with the equally indispensable 'reasons of the heart', as Pascal would say. For the Church, man is neither mere reason nor mere feeling, he is the unity of these two dimensions. The head must reflect with lucidity, but the heart must be able to feel warmth: devotion to Mary (which 'avoids every false exaggeration on the one hand, and excessive narrow-mindedness in the contemplation of the surpassing dignity of the Mother of God on the other', as the Council urges) thus assures the faith its full human dimension."

Continuing his synthesis, Ratzinger lists a *fifth* point: "To use the very formulations of Vatican II, Mary is 'figure', 'image' and 'model' of the Church. Beholding her the Church is shielded against the aforementioned masculinized model that views her as an instrument for a program of social-political action. In Mary, as figure and archetype, the Church again finds her own visage as Mother and cannot degenerate into the complexity of a party, an organization or a pressure group in the service of human interests, even the noblest. If Mary no longer finds a place in many theologies and ecclesiologies, the reason is obvious: they have reduced faith to an abstraction. And an abstraction does not need a Mother."

Here is the *sixth* and last point of this synthesis: "With her destiny, which is at one and the same time that of Virgin and of Mother, Mary continues to project a light upon that which the Creator intended for women in every age, ours included, or, better said, perhaps precisely in our time, in which—as we know—the very essence of femininity is threatened. Through her virginity and her motherhood, the mystery of woman receives a very lofty destiny from which she cannot be torn away. Mary undauntedly proclaims the

Magnificat, but she is also the one who renders silence and seclusion fruitful. She is the one who does not fear to stand under the Cross, who is present at the birth of the Church. But she is also the one who, as the evangelist emphasizes more than once, 'keeps and ponders in her heart' that which transpires around her. As a creature of courage and of obedience she was and is still an example to which every Christian — man and woman — can and should look."

Fatima and environs

One of the four sections of the Congregation for the Doctrine of the Faith (the so-called disciplinary section) is entrusted with the task of judging Marian apparitions.

I ask: "Cardinal Ratzinger, have you read the so-called 'third secret of Fatima', which Sister Lucia, the only survivor of the group of those who beheld the apparition, forwarded to Pope John XXIII, and which the Pope, after he had examined it, passed on to your predecessor, Cardinal Ottaviani, ordering him to deposit it in the archives of the Holy Office?"

The reply is immediate and dry: "Yes, I have read it."

Undenied versions are circulating in the world, I continue, which describe the contents of that "secret" as disquieting, apocalyptic, as warning of terrible sufferings. John Paul II himself, in his personal visit to Germany, seemed to confirm (albeit with prudent circumlocutions, privately, to a select group) the undeniably disconcerting contents of that text. Before him, Paul VI, during his pilgrimage to Fatima, also seems to have alluded to the "apocalyptic" themes of the "secret". Why was it never decided to make it public, if only to counter rash speculations?

"If this decision has not yet been made", he answers, "it is not because the Popes want to hide something terrible."

Then there is "something terrible" in Sister Lucia's manuscript, I insist?

"If that were so", he replies, avoiding going further, "that after all would only confirm the part of the message of Fatima already known. A stern warning has been launched from that place that is directed against the prevailing frivolity, a summons to the seriousness of life, of history, to the perils that threaten humanity. It is that which Jesus himself recalls very frequently: '. . . Unless you repent you will all perish . . .' (Lk 13:3). Conversion—and Fatima fully recalls it to mind—is a constant demand of Christian life. We should already know that from the whole of sacred Scripture."

So there will be no publication, at least for now?

"The Holy Father deems that it would add nothing to what a Christian must know from Revelation and also from the Marian apparitions approved by the Church in their known contents, which only reconfirmed the urgency of penance, conversion, forgiveness, fasting. To publish the 'third secret' would mean exposing the Church to the danger of sensationalism, exploitation of the content."

Perhaps also political implications, I venture, since it seems that here, also, as in the two other "secrets", Russia is mentioned?

At this point, however, the Cardinal declares that he is not in a position to go further into the matter and firmly refuses to discuss other particulars. On the other hand, at the time of our interview, the Pope proceeded to reconsecrate the world (with a particular mention of Eastern Europe) to the Immaculate Heart of Mary, precisely in accordance with the exhortation of the Virgin of Fatima, and the same John Paul II, wounded by his would-be assassin, on May 13—anniversary of the first apparition in the Portuguese locality—went to Fatima in order to thank Mary, "whose hand (he said) had miraculously guided the bullet", and seemed to refer to the forewarnings that had been transmitted through a group of children to humanity and that seemed to refer also to the person of the Pontiff.

On the same theme, it is well known that for years, now, a village in Yugoslavia, Medjugorje, is at the center of world attention because of reported "apparitions" which—whether true or not—have already drawn millions of pilgrims. But they have also provoked deplorable conflicts between the Franciscans who govern the parish and the bishop of the local diocese. Is a clarifying statement of the Congregation for the Doctrine of the Faith, the highest court in this matter, to be expected, with, of course, the approval of the Pope, which is indispensable for each one of its documents?

He replies: "In this area, more than ever, patience is the fundamental principle of the policy of our Congregation. No apparition is indispensable to the faith; Revelation terminated with Jesus Christ. He himself is the Revelation. But we certainly cannot prevent God from speaking to our time through simple persons and also through extraordinary signs that point to the insufficiency of the cultures stamped by rationalism and positivism that dominate us. The apparitions that the Church has officially approved—especially Lourdes and Fatima—have their precise place in the development of the life of the Church in the last century. They show, among other things, that Revelation—still unique, concluded and therefore unsurpassable—is not yet a dead thing but something alive and vital. Moreover—prescinding Medjugorje, on which I cannot express a judgment since the case is still being examined by the Congregation— one of the signs of our times is that the announcements of

'Marian apparitions' are multiplying all over the world. For example, reports are arriving from Africa and from other continents at the section of the Congregation that is competent to deal with such reports."

But, I ask, besides the traditional element of patience and prudence, on what criteria does the Congregation base itself for a judgment, in the face of the multiplication of these facts?

"One of our criteria", he says, "is to separate the aspect of the true or presumed 'supernaturality' of the apparition from that of its spiritual fruits. The pilgrimages of ancient Christianity were often concentrated on places with respect to which our modern critical spirit would be horrified as to the 'scientific truth' of the tradition bound up with them. This does not detract from the fact that those pilgrimages were fruitful, beneficial, rich in blessings and important for the life of the Christian people. The problem is not so much that of modern hypercriticism (which ends up later, moreover, in a form of new credulity), but it is that of the evaluation of the vitality and of the orthodoxy of the religious life that is developing around these places."

CHAPTER EIGHT

A SPIRITUALITY FOR TODAY

Faith and the body

Whether or not they are recognized as real, the "messages of the Marian apparitions" are problematic also because they seem to go in a direction hardly consonant with certain "post-conciliar spiritualities".

He interrupts me: "I want to emphasize that I don't like the terms *pre-* or *post-*conciliar. To accept them would be tantamount to accepting a rupture in the history of the Church. In the 'apparitions' the inclusion of the body (signs of the cross, holy water, call to fasting) often plays a special role, but all this is fully in line with Vatican II, which insisted upon the unity of man, hence upon the incarnation of the spirit in the flesh."

That fasting to which you allude seems actually to occupy a central position in many of those "messages".

"Fasting means to accept an essential aspect of Christian life. It is necessary to rediscover the corporeal aspect of the Faith: abstention from food is one of those aspects. Sexuality and nourishment are among the fundamental elements of the physicality of man. In our time, the decline in the understanding of virginity goes hand in hand with the decline in the understanding of fasting. And these two declines have a single root: the present-day eclipse of the eschatological tension, that is, the tension of Christian faith toward eternal life. Virginity and periodic abstinence from food are meant to testify that eternal life awaits us, indeed that it is already among us, and 'the form of this world passes away' (1 Cor 7:31). Without virginity and without fasting the Church is no longer Church, she is assimilated to her historical surroundings. This is why we must look to the example of our brethren of the Eastern Orthodox churches, great teachers — even today — of authentic Christian asceticism."

Your Eminence, if the "corporeal forms of expression" of the faith are disappearing among Catholics (surviving, perhaps, among restricted cloistered elites), the orientation of the institutional Church has had a role in it: through a series of measures coming from Rome, Friday abstinence, vigils, Advent and other special times of fasting have been mitigated.

"True, but the intention was good", he says. "It was a matter of eliminating suspicions of legalism, of temptations to transform religion into external practices. What certainly remains is that fasting, abstinence and other penances must continue to be linked to personal responsibility. But it is also important that we find the way back to common expressions of ecclesial penance. Beyond that, in a world in many parts of which people are dying of hunger, we must again bear a visible and communal witness of an abstention from food, accepted freely, for love."

Different with respect to the "world"

In his view, however, the problem is more comprehensive: "Here, too, we must rediscover the courage of nonconformism in the face of the trends of the affluent world. Instead of following the spirit of the times, we ourselves must witness that spirit of nonconformity with evangelical seriousness. We have lost the sense that Christians cannot live just like 'everybody else'. The foolish idea according to which there is no specific Christian morality is only an expression of the loss of a basic concept: what is 'distinctively Christian' with respect to the models of the 'world'. Even in some religious orders and congregations true reform has been exchanged for the relaxation of traditional austerity until then in practice. *Renewal* has been exchanged for *comfort*. To cite a small but concrete example: a religious reported to me that the ruin of his monastery had begun — very concretely — when it was declared that rising for the recitation of the nocturnal office was 'no longer practicable'. Well, this uncontested but significant 'sacrifice' has been replaced by TV-viewing until well into the night. A seemingly trivial matter, but the present-day decline of the indispensable austerity of Christian life is fashioned also by these 'trivial' matters, beginning with the members of the religious orders."

He continues his train of thought: "Today more than ever the Christian must be aware that he belongs to a minority and that he is in opposition to everything that appears good, obvious, logical to the 'spirit of the world', as the New Testament calls it. Among the most urgent tasks facing Christians is that of regaining the capacity of nonconformism, i.e., the capacity to oppose many developments of the surrounding culture. In other words, today we must revise this euphoric view of the early post-conciliar era."

Can, then, the *Imitation of Christ* continue to exist alongside *Gaudium et spes*?

"Obviously, it is a matter of two very different spiritualities. The *Imitation* is a text that reflects the great late medieval monastic tradition. But Vatican II in no way intended to take good things away from the good."

And is the *Imitation of Christ* (taken, of course, as a symbol of a certain spirituality) still among the "good" things?

"Indeed: among the most urgent objectives of the modern Catholic belongs that of recovering all the positive elements of a spirituality of this kind, with its awareness of the qualitative distance between the mentality of faith and a worldly mentality. To be sure, in the *Imitation* there is a one-sided emphasis on the private relationship of the Christian with the Lord. But in too much of the contemporary theological production there is an insufficient understanding of spiritual interiority. Its global and irrevocable condemnation of the *fuga seculi* (flight from the world), which is at the center of classic spirituality, failed to perceive that there was also a social aspect to that 'flight'. One fled the world, not to abandon it to itself, but in order to find in places of recollection new possibilities of Christian and, therefore, human existence. One acquired a clear perception of the alienation of society, and in the hermitages and in the monasteries new social models based on new foundations were tested. Oases of true life arose in the desert; one gathered fresh hope for the salvation of all."

Just consider: twenty years ago it was declared in sundry tones that the most pressing problem of the Catholic was to find a spirituality that was "new", "communitarian", "open", "non-sacral", "turned toward the world". Now after long wanderings it is being discovered that the urgent task is to find again a connecting link with the ancient spirituality of "flight from the world".

"The problem", he responds, "is once more that of finding a new equilibrium. Apart from the legitimate, indeed, for the Church, precious monastic or eremitic vocations, the believer is held to live that none-too-easy balance between a proper incarnation in history and the indispensable tension toward eternity. It is precisely this balance that prevents one from either sacralizing earthly commitment or laying oneself open to the reproach of 'alienation'."

The challenge of the sects

Almost all the sects that continue to spread among the ex-faithful of the "official" Christian churches are characterized by an eschatological emphasis, flight from the world, agitated calls to a "change of life", to conversion, to coinvolvement of the body (abstinence from alcohol, from tobacco, often from meat, the most varied kinds of "sacrifice"). From year to year the phenomenon is assuming ever more impressive dimensions: is there a common strategy of the Church in order to counter this advance?

"There are individual initiatives on the part of bishops and episcopates", the Prefect replies. "Doubtlessly we will have to establish a line of common action between the episcopal conferences and competent organs of the Holy See, and so far as possible with other important ecclesial communities. It must be said, however, that Christianity has always and everywhere known religious marginal groups which were exposed to the fascination of this kind of eccentric and heterodox preaching."

Now, however, it seems that these "marginal" manifestations seem to be transforming themselves into a mass phenomenon.

"Their spread", he says, "also points to some lacunae and shortcomings in our preaching and practice. For example: the radical eschatologism, the millenarism that is typical of many of these sects can make headway also thanks to the disappearance of this genuinely Catholic aspect in many areas of the pastoral ministry. There is in these sects a sensibility (carried to extremes, but which is authentically Christian when in a balanced measure) vis-à-vis the perils of our time and, therefore, to the possibility of an imminent end of history. The correct evaluation of messages such as those of Fatima can represent one form of our answer: the Church hearkening to the message of Christ, delivered through Mary to our time, feels the threat to all and to each individual and responds with a decisive conversion and penance."

In the Cardinal's view, however, the most radical response to the sects will follow from a "rediscovery of Catholic identity". "A new clarity is necessary, a new joy, if one can put it thus, a new 'pride' (which does not contradict the necessary humility) in being Catholic. It must be borne in mind that these groups also reap success because they offer to people, increasingly more alone, isolated and uncertain, a kind of 'homeland of the soul' and the warmth of a community. It is precisely this warmth and this life which, unfortunately, seem often to be lacking with us: in places where the parishes, that indispensable matrix, have understood how to revitalize themselves and to offer the sense of the little church that lives in union with the great Church, the sectarians have hardly been able to gain ground in a significant way. Our catechesis then must unmask the point on which these new 'missionaries' harp: the impression, namely, that Scripture is to be read in a 'literal' sense, while Catholics assertedly have weakened or forgotten it. This *literalness* often signifies a betrayal of *fidelity*. The isolation of single sentences and verses is misleading and loses sight of the whole. Read as a whole, the Bible is really 'Catholic'. But this must first be shown through a catechetical instruction that would rehabituate the faithful to a reading of sacred Scripture in and with the Church."

CHAPTER NINE

LITURGY:

BETWEEN OLD AND NEW

Saving the riches

Cardinal, let us talk a little about the liturgy and liturgical reform, one of the most debated and most embarrassing problems. It is one of the bones of contention of the traditionalist anti-conciliar movement, and of the pathetic integralism of a Msgr. Marcel Lefebvre. Archbishop Lefebvre is in revolt especially on account of certain liturgical innovations in which he senses the sulfurous smell of heresy. . . .

He interrupts me to clarify something: "With regard to particular concrete modes of liturgical reform, and above all with regard to the positions adopted by particular liturgists, the feeling of unease extends far beyond the corridors of integralism. In other words, not every one who expresses such unease must necessarily be an integralist."

Do you mean perhaps that even a Catholic who is far removed from extreme traditionalism would be right to be suspicious of, or even to protest against, a certain kind of post-conciliar liturgism? I am not speaking of a Catholic who has got stuck in nostalgia, but of a person who is willing to accept Vatican II in its entirety.

"Behind the various ways of understanding liturgy there are," he answers, "as almost always, different ways of understanding the Church and consequently God and man's

relation to him. The question of liturgy is not peripheral:
the Council itself reminded us that we are dealing here with
the very core of Christian faith."

His important tasks in Rome mean that Joseph Ratzinger
has neither time nor opportunity to go on publishing scholarly articles and books as he would like to. The fact that one
of the few books he has published in these years is on the
theme of liturgy (*Das Fest des Glaubens* [*The Feast of Faith*])
shows how important the topic of liturgy is to him. This
book is a collection of short essays on the liturgy, and in it
he deals with a particular understanding of *aggiornamento*
about which he had already expressed deep concern ten years
after the end of the Council.

I take out that passage from 1975 and read it to him: "It
was right and proper to open up the liturgy to the vernacular;
even the Council of Trent saw it as a possibility. Furthermore
it is simply untrue to say, as certain integralists do, that drawing up new forms of the Canon of the Mass is a contradiction
of Trent. For the present we cannot go into the question of
how far specific steps taken by the liturgical reform were real
improvements or actually trivializations, how far they were
wise or foolish or reckless from a pastoral point of view."[1]

I continue reading from the article by Joseph Ratzinger, at
that time still a professor of theology but already a member of
the international papal theological commission: "One thing
is clear: however much the liturgy is simplified and rendered
comprehensible, the mystery of God's action operating
through the Church's acts must remain untouched. This applies also to the heart of the liturgy: as far as both priest and
people are concerned, it is something given, that cannot be
manipulated. It partakes of the reality of the whole Church."[2]

[1] Quoted from *Thesen zum Thema 'Zehn Jahre Vaticanum II'* (typescript).
[2] Ibid.

"It follows", urges Professor Ratzinger, "that we must be far more resolute than heretofore in opposing rationalistic relativism, confusing claptrap and pastoral infantilism. These things degrade the liturgy to the level of a parish tea party and the intelligibility of the popular newspaper. With this in mind we shall also have to examine the reforms already carried out, particularly in the area of the *Rituale*."[3]

As I read these observations back to him, he listens with his accustomed attention and patience. Ten years have gone by, and the author of this admonitory call is no longer an ordinary scholar: he is a guardian precisely of the Church's orthodoxy. Does the Ratzinger of today, the Prefect of the Congregation for the Faith, recognize himself in these words?

"Absolutely", he replies without hesitation. "Moreover, since I wrote those lines, other aspects which should have been guarded have been neglected; many treasures that were still intact have been squandered away. Then, in 1975, many of my theological colleagues were upset or at least surprised by what I said. Now many of those same people admit that I was right, at least in part."

So further misinterpretations and errors have arisen, justifying all the more the grave words in the book to which we have referred, which appeared six years later: "One shudders at the lackluster face of the post-conciliar liturgy as it has become, or one is simply bored with its hankering after banality and its lack of artistic standards. . . ."[4]

[3] Ibid.
[4] *Das Fest des Glaubens*, 88.

The language, for example . . .

In his view it is precisely the area of liturgy, both in the work of experts and in practical applications, that is "one of the clearest examples of the contrast between what the authentic text of Vatican II says and the way in which it has been understood and applied."

An example that is only too familiar and exposed to abuse is the use of Latin, on which the Council clearly says, "The use of the Latin language, with due respect to particular law, is to be preserved in the Latin rites" (*Sacrosanctum concilium*, no. 36). Lower down the Fathers urge, "Nevertheless, care must be taken to ensure that the faithful may also be able to say or sing in Latin those parts of the Ordinary of the Mass which pertain to them" (*Sacrosanctum concilium*, no. 54). Further on in the same document we read, "In accordance with the age-old tradition of the Latin rite, the Latin language is to be retained by clerics in the divine office" (no. 101).

As we said at the outset, the aim of this conversation with Cardinal Ratzinger was not to focus on our own opinions but to report on the views of the interviewee. Yet, although it may seem a small matter, personally we find it a rather strange attitude on the part of those who mourn like "widows" and "orphans" for a past that has gone forever. We feel no nostalgia for a Latin liturgy which we only knew in its last and exhausted phase. However, reading the Council documents, one can understand Cardinal Ratzinger's concern: it is an objective fact that, even if we restrict ourselves to the issue of the liturgical language, there is a striking contrast between the texts of Vatican II and the practical consequences which followed in the wake of the Council. Our aim is not to lament and complain, but to learn from an authoritative source how this dichotomy has come about.

He shakes his head: "This is another of those cases which are all too frequent in recent years, where there is a contradiction between, on the one hand, what the Council actually says, the authentic structure of the Church and her worship, the real, contemporary pastoral requirements, and, on the other hand, the concrete response of particular clerical circles. But the language of the liturgy was never a side issue. At the beginning of the break between the Latin West and the Greek East there was also a problem of a linguistic lack of mutual understanding. This disappearance of a common liturgical language could possibly increase the centrifugal forces at work in the different Catholic regions." But he immediately adds, "In order to explain the rapid and almost total abandonment of the ancient, common liturgical language, we must also take into account a fundamental cultural change in Western public education. Even in the early sixties when I was a professor, it was possible to read a Latin text to young people coming straight from German secondary schools. Nowadays this is no longer possible."

"Pluralism, but for all"

Apropos of the Latin language: at the time when our conversation was taking place, word had not come through of the Pope's decision (dated October 3, 1984, and signed by the Pro-Prefect of the Congregation of Rites) regarding the controversial "Indult" permitting priests to celebrate Mass in Latin according to the Roman Missal of 1962. This signifies the possibility of an (albeit clearly circumscribed) return to the pre-conciliar language, "but it must be publicly made clear", the document goes on, "that the priests and faithful concerned in no way share the view of those who question the legitimacy and doctrinal reliability of the Roman Missal promulgated by Pope Paul VI in 1979",[5] and only if the celebration according to the old rite "takes place in churches and chapels appointed by the bishop and not in parish churches, unless the local bishop permits it by way of exception."[6] In spite of these restrictions and stern warnings ("the granting of the Indult may in no way be used as an obstacle to faithful observance of liturgical reform"),[7] the Pope's decision has resulted in polemics.

We too—in all honesty—were taken aback. But we must mention something that Cardinal Ratzinger said to us in Brixen: although he made no reference to this new measure —which was evidently already decided and of which he no doubt had been informed—he had indicated that something of the sort might be possible. Far from regarding this "Indult" on the lines of a "restoration", he saw it rather in the context of that "legitimate pluralism" which has been so stressed by Vatican II and its interpreters.

Let us hear the Cardinal himself: "Prior to Trent a multiplicity of rites and liturgies had been allowed within the Church. The Fathers of Trent took the liturgy of the city of Rome and prescribed it for the whole Church; they only retained those Western liturgies which had existed for more than two hundred years. This is what happened, for instance, with the Ambrosian rite of the Diocese of Milan. If it would foster devotion in many believers and encourage respect for the piety of particular Catholic groups, I would personally support a return to the ancient situation, i.e., to a certain liturgical pluralism. Provided, of course, that the legitimate character of the reformed rites was emphatically affirmed, and that there was a clear delineation of the extent

[5] Document of the Congregation for the Faith of October 3, 1984.
[6] Ibid.
[7] Ibid.

and nature of such an exception permitting the celebration of the pre-conciliar liturgy." This was no doubt more than a personal wish on his part, since it was realized in hardly less than a month.

In any case he himself has reminded us, in his *Feast of Faith*, that, where liturgy is concerned, as elsewhere, "*Catholicity* does not mean *uniformity*", and he points out that, "It is strange that the post-conciliar pluralism has created uniformity in one respect at least: it will not tolerate a high standard of expression. We need to counter this by reinstating the whole range of possibilities within the unity of the Catholic liturgy."[8]

A space for the sacred

Let us return to the general issue: what does the Prefect object to in certain contemporary liturgies? (Or perhaps it is not so much contemporary liturgy that is at fault, for, as he observes, "it seems that certain abuses associated with the post conciliar years are lessening. . . . It seems to me that a reconciliation is in process, and some people are becoming aware that they went too far and too fast." "But", he adds, for the present this new equilibrium only affects an elite group, it is only to be found in certain circles of experts, whereas the whole wave set in motion by them is only now reaching the generality of the faithful. So it comes about that many a priest or layman, late in the day, gets enthusiastic about something — regards it as 'avant-garde' — that the experts were putting forward yesterday, whereas now these same experts have moved on to different, and maybe even more traditional, positions.")

What needs to be discovered in an entirely new way, according to Ratzinger, is the "given, nonarbitrary, 'constant'

[8] *Das Fest des Glaubens,* 108.

and 'unshakable' character of liturgical worship." He recalls that "there were years when the faithful wondered, as they prepared themselves to participate in a rite or in the Mass itself, what form the celebrant's 'creativity' would take that day. . . ." This is something, he reminds us, that also contradicts the uncommonly strict and solemn exhortation of the Council: "Regulation of the sacred liturgy depends solely on the authority of the Church, that is, on the Apostolic See and, as laws may determine, on the bishop. . . . Therefore no other person, not even a priest, may add, remove, or change anything in the liturgy on his own authority" (*Sacrosanctum concilium*, no. 22, 1 and 3).

He says, "The liturgy is not a show, a spectacle, requiring brilliant producers and talented actors. The life of the liturgy does not consist in 'pleasant' surprises and attractive 'ideas' but in solemn repetitions. It cannot be an expression of what is current and transitory, for it expresses the mystery of the Holy. Many people have felt and said that liturgy must be 'made' by the whole community if it is really to belong to them. Such an attitude has led to the 'success' of the liturgy being measured by its effect at the level of spectacle and entertainment. It is to lose sight of what is *distinctive* to the liturgy, which does not come from what *we do* but from the fact that something is *taking place* here that all of us together cannot 'make'. In the liturgy there is a power, an energy at work which not even the Church as a whole can generate: what it manifests is the Wholly Other, coming to us through the community (which is hence not sovereign but servant, purely instrumental)."

He goes on: "Liturgy, for the Catholic, is his common homeland, the source of his identity. And another reason why it must be something 'given' and 'constant' is that, by means of the ritual, it manifests the holiness of God. The revolt against what has been described as 'the old rubricist rigidity', which was accused of stifling 'creativity', has in fact made the liturgy into a do-it-yourself patchwork and trivialized it, adapting it to our mediocrity."

Ratzinger wanted to point out another area of problems: "The Council rightly reminded us that liturgy also means *actio*, something done, and it demanded that the faithful be guaranteed an *actuosa participatio*, an active participation."

I regard that as a very good thing, I observe.

"Certainly", he agrees. "The concept is no doubt correct. But the way it has been applied following the Council has exhibited a fatal narrowing of perspective. The impression arose that there was only 'active participation' when there was discernible external activity — speaking, singing, preaching, reading, shaking hands. It was forgotten that the Council also included silence under *actuosa participatio*, for silence facilitates a really deep, personal participation, allowing us to listen inwardly to the Lord's word. Many liturgies now lack all trace of this silence."

Sounds and images for the Eternal

At this point he comes to speak directly about church music, that traditional music of the Catholic West which Vatican II praised in generous terms, urging those responsible not only to preserve it with "the greatest care" but to cultivate what it calls the "Church's treasury", which is also a treasury for the whole of humanity. But what has in fact happened?

"Instead many liturgists have thrust this treasure aside, calling it 'esoteric' and treating it slightingly in the name of an 'intelligibility for all and at every moment, which ought to characterize the post-conciliar liturgy'. Thus instead of 'church music'—which is banished to cathedrals for special occasions—we only have 'utility music', songs, easy melodies, catchy tunes."

Here too the Cardinal has no difficulty in illustrating how, both in theoretical and practical terms, people have moved away from the Council, "which regarded sacred music as actual liturgy, and not mere additional ornamentation." It would be easy to show, he says, how "the surrender of the beautiful" has in fact resulted in a "pastoral defeat".

He says: "More and more clearly we can discern the frightening impoverishment which takes place when people show beauty the door and devote themselves exclusively to 'utility'. Experience has shown that the retreat to 'intelligibility for all', taken as the sole criterion, does not really make liturgies more intelligible and more open but only poorer. 'Simple' liturgy does not mean poor or cheap liturgy: there is the simplicity of the banal and the simplicity that comes from spiritual, cultural and historical wealth." He continues: "Here too they have pushed the great church music aside in the name of 'active participation', but cannot this 'participation' also include receptivity on the part of the spirit and the senses? Is there really nothing 'active' in perceiving, receiving and being inwardly moved? This is surely a diminution of man, a reduction to what can be expressed in speech, in spite of the fact that nowadays we know that what we are rationally conscious of, what comes to the surface, is only the tip of the iceberg compared with the totality of the human being. In questioning this approach, we are not, of course, opposing the efforts being made to encourage the whole congregation to sing, nor are we against 'utility music' in itself. But what we must oppose is the exclusivity which insists on *that* music alone and which is justified neither by the Council nor by pastoral necessity."

This discussion of church music — which he also sees as the symbol of the presence in the Church of a beauty which is *gratis*, calling for our grateful response — is something dear to the heart of Joseph Ratzinger. He has written gripping pages on this subject: "A Church which only makes use of 'utility music' has fallen for what is, in fact, useless and becomes useless herself. For her mission is a far higher one. As the Old Testament speaks of the Temple, the Church is to be the place of 'glory' and, as such, too, the place where mankind's cry of distress is brought to the ear of God. The Church must not settle down with what is merely comfortable and serviceable at the parish level; she must arouse the voice of the cosmos and, by glorifying the Creator, elicit the glory of the cosmos itself, making it too glorious, beautiful, habitable and beloved."[9]

Here too, however, as in regard to Latin, he speaks of a "cultural upheaval", even of an almost "anthropological change" particularly in the case of young people, "whose musical sense has been stunted since the beginning of the sixties by rock music and related forms." This has gone so far (and here he refers to his pastoral experience in Germany) that nowadays "it is hard to persuade young people to listen to the old German hymns, let alone sing them."

This realization of the objective difficulties does not stop him, however, from making a passionate defense not only of music but of Christian art in general and of its function of revealing truth: "The only really effective apologia for Christianity comes down to two arguments, namely, the *saints* the Church has produced and the *art* which has grown in her womb. Better witness is borne to the Lord by the splendor of holiness and art which have arisen in the community of believers than by the clever excuses which apologetics has come up with to justify the dark sides which, sadly, are so frequent in the Church's human history. If the Church is to continue to transform and humanize the world, how can she dispense with beauty in her liturgies, that beauty which is so closely linked with love and with the radiance of the Resurrection? No. Christians must not be too easily satisfied. They must make their Church into a place where beauty—and hence truth—is at home. Without this the world will become the first circle of hell."

He tells me of a famous theologian, one of the leading figures of post-conciliar thought, who admitted without a qualm that he felt himself to be a "barbarian". He comments: "A theologian who does not love art, poetry, music and nature can be dangerous. Blindness and deafness toward the beautiful are not incidental: they necessarily are reflected in his theology."

Solemnity, not triumphalism

In this respect too, Ratzinger is by no means impressed by the cries of "triumphalism!" which accompanied the wanton jettisoning of much of the old solemnity: "In the solemnity of the worship, the Church expressed the glory of God, the joy of faith, the victory of truth and light over error and darkness. The richness of the liturgy is not the richness of some priestly caste: it is the wealth of all, including the poor, who in fact long for it and do not at all find it a stumbling block. The whole history of popular piety shows that the poorest have always been instinctively and spontaneously ready even to do without necessities in order to show honor through beauty to their Lord and God without giving any thought to themselves."

As an example he cites something he experienced on one of his last visits to North America: "The authorities of the Anglican Church in New York had decided to cease work on the new Cathedral. They felt that it was too magnificent and constituted an affront to the people, to whom they had decided to distribute the money that had been collected. And it was precisely the poor who refused to accept the money and called for the work to be recommenced; they could not understand the strange idea that the worship of God could be subject to calculation and that one could dispense with solemnity and beauty when standing in his presence."

If I have understood him correctly, the Cardinal's accusation is directed against certain Christian intellectuals, against a particular framework of thought which is peculiar to them, aristocratic and elitist in tone, and far removed from what the "People of God" really believes and longs for: "A certain kind of modern neoclericalism sees man's problem as his sense of being oppressed by 'sacred taboos'. This is, however, the problem of those clerics who are going through a crisis. The drama faced by our contemporaries is rather that of living without hope in an ever more profane world. Nowadays the really widespread demand is not for a secularized liturgy but, on the contrary, for a new encounter with the sacred through a worship that manifests the presence of the Eternal."

He also objects to something else, however, namely, "the romantic archaeologism of certain professors of liturgy who would throw out everything done after Gregory the Great as being an excrescence and a sign of decadence. For them, the criterion of liturgical renewal was not *'What ought to be done today?'* but *'What was it like then?'* They forget that the Church is living and that her liturgy cannot be frozen at the stage reached in the city of Rome prior to the onset of the Middle Ages. In reality the medieval Church (or the Church of the Baroque era, in many respects) developed a liturgical depth which must be carefully examined before it is abandoned. Here too we must be aware of the Catholic law of an ever better and deeper insight into the inheritance entrusted to us. Pure archaism is fruitless, as is pure modernization."

Thus, for Ratzinger, the life of worship of the Catholic must not be restricted to the merely "communal" aspect: there must also be room for personal piety, even though it is ordered to the common prayer, i.e., the liturgy.

Eucharist at the heart of the faith

He adds: "Some apparently see liturgy narrowly in terms of the Eucharist alone, and only under the aspect of the 'brotherly meal'. But the Mass is not only a meal among friends who have come together to remember the Lord's Last Supper through the common breaking of bread. The Mass is the common sacrifice of the Church, in which the Lord prays with us and for us and communicates himself to us. It is the sacramental renewal of Christ's sacrifice: consequently its redeeming power extends to all men, those present and those far away, the living and the dead. We need to rediscover the awareness that the Eucharist is not worthless if one does not receive communion: such an awareness would do a great deal to lighten the burden of such acute problems as the readmission to communion of the divorced and remarried." I asked him to explain further: "If the Eucharist is only experienced as a community meal among friends, the person who is excluded from receiving the sacred gifts really is cut off from the brotherhood. But if we return to the full perspective of the Mass (a brotherly meal, but also the Lord's sacrifice, carrying *within it* its own power and effect for the person who is united with him in faith), even if a person does not eat that 'bread', he still shares equally in all the other gifts made available."

One of the first official documents of the Congregation for the Faith to bear his signature was devoted by Cardinal Ratzinger to the Eucharist and the issues surrounding its "minister". (The latter can only be a person consecrated in the "ministerial, i.e., hierarchical priesthood", which, as the Council again affirms, is different "essentially and not only in degree" from "the common priesthood of the faithful": *Lumen Gentium*, no. 10.) In "the attempt to separate the Eucharist from the necessary link with the hierarchical priesthood", Ratzinger sees another aspect of the "trivializing" of the sacramental mystery.

The same danger is present here as in the decline in adoration before the Blessed Sacrament: "People have forgotten that adoration is an intensification of communion. It is not a case of 'individualistic' piety: it is a prolonging of, or a preparation for, the community element. The *Corpus Christi* processions so loved by the people should be retained. (When I led them in Munich, tens of thousands of people took part.) Here again the liturgical 'archaeologists' voice their objections and point out that these processions did not exist in the Roman Church in the first centuries. But I repeat what I said before, we must recognize that the *sensus fidei* of the Catholic people is able, as the centuries proceed, to draw forth all the consequences of the inheritance entrusted to them, to plumb that inheritance and bring it into the light of day."

"Not only the Mass"

He goes on: "The Eucharist is the central core of our liturgical life, but for it to be the center, we need a shared total context in which to live. All investigations of the effects of the liturgical reform show that if the Mass is over-emphasized pastorally, it becomes devalued. It is placed in a vacuum, as it were, without other liturgical acts to prepare for it or deepen it. The Eucharist presupposes the other sacraments and points toward them. But Eucharist also presupposes personal prayer, prayer in the family and extra-liturgical prayer in community."

What are you thinking of here?

"I am thinking of two of the deepest and most fruitful prayers of Christendom, which are always leading us anew into the mighty river of the Eucharist: the *Stations of the Cross* and the *Rosary*. If nowadays we are so dangerously exposed to the attractions of Asiatic religious practices, it is surely in part because we have forgotten these prayers." He observes, "If the Rosary is prayed as tradition envisages, it draws us into a rhythm of calm which makes us flexible and well balanced, giving a name to this peace: Jesus, the blessed fruit of Mary. Mary, who kept the living Word in the quiet peace of her heart and so was able to become mother of the Incarnate Word. That is why Mary is the ideal of genuine liturgical life. She is Mother of the Church, and as such she also shows us the task and the highest goal of our worship: the glory of God, from whom mankind's salvation comes."

LE 5-4050

THE PARACLETE
BOOK CENTER

146 EAST 74th STREET
NEW YORK, NEW YORK 10021

| ACCT. | | | | | | |

Customer's
Order No._____ Date___ JAN 2 86 19___

Name_____

Address_____

SOLD BY	CASH	C.O.D.	CHARGE	ON ACCT.	MDSE. RETD.	PAID OUT	
	✓						

QUAN	DESCRIPTION	PRICE	AMOUNT
	Ratzinger Report	9.95	
			82
	Thank You!		$ 10.77
		TOTAL	

All claims and returned goods **MUST** be accompanied by this bill.   5103

619881   Rec'd By_____

CHAPTER TEN

ON SOME "LAST THINGS"

The devil and his trail

Among the many things Cardinal Ratzinger has told me and which have been reported prior to the publication of this book, there is one area which, while it is not absolutely central, has evidently attracted the attention of very many commentators. As could be expected, many articles (and their corresponding titles) were devoted not so much to the strictly theological, exegetical and ecclesiological statements of the Prefect of the Congregation for the Faith as to remarks made—a few paragraphs, totaling perhaps ten pages— concerning that reality to which Christian tradition applies the terms *"devil"*, *"demon"* and *"Satan"*.

Does this show a liking for the picturesque, a curiosity about something which many people (Christians too) regard as a "vestigial piece of folklore", as something which is at all events "unacceptable to mature faith"? Or is there perhaps something deeper behind it; uneasiness beneath a veneer of laughter? Is this urbane lightheartedness, or is it an exorcism in the cloak of irony?

It is not for us to give an answer. But it is a fact that no other topic unleashes such a storm of indignation among the mass-media of secularized society as that of the "devil".

It is hard to forget the widely reverberating echo—which was not merely ironic but occasionally furious—provoked by Pope Paul VI. During his general audience of November 15, 1972, he took up a subject he had raised on June 29 of that year in St. Peter's, when, speaking of the Church's situation, he said, "I have the feeling that the smoke of Satan has penetrated the Temple of God through some crack or other." He added that, "since we find reference to this enemy of mankind so frequently in the mouth of Christ in the Gospel", he, Paul VI, believed even today "in something supernatural that has come into the world to destroy and strangle the very fruits of the Ecumenical Council and to stop the Church from breaking out into a hymn of joy, by sowing doubt, uncertainty, problems, unrest and discontent".[1]

These first indications immediately raised a suppressed protest throughout the world. It burst forth fully—and lasted for months in all the world's media—on that famous November 15, 1972: "The evil which exists in the world is the result and effect of an attack upon us and our society by a dark and hostile agent, the devil. Evil is not only a privation but a living, spiritual, corrupt and corrupting being. A terrible reality, mysterious and frightening. The testimony of both Bible and Church tells us that people refuse to acknowledge his existence; or they make of him a self-subsistent principle not originating in God, unlike all creatures; or he is explained away as a pseudo-reality, a fantastic personification of the unknown grounds of the evil within us."[2]

After adducing a series of biblical quotations in support of his statement, Paul VI continued: "The devil is the enemy number one, the source of all temptation. Thus we know that this dark and destructive being really exists and is still active; he is the sophistical perverter of man's moral equipoise,

[1] Paul VI, General Audience, June 29, 1972.
[2] Paul VI, Address, November 15, 1972.

the malicious seducer who knows how to penetrate us (through the senses, the imagination, desire, utopian logic or disordered social contacts) in order to spread error. . . ."[3]

The Pope went on to regret that contemporary theology lacked an awareness of this problem: "It would be very important to return to a study of Catholic teaching on the devil and the influence he is able to wield, but nowadays little attention is paid to it."[4] The Congregation for the Faith then took up the theme in the document of June 1975, evidently in defense of the teaching affirmed by the Pope: "Teaching concerning the devil is an undisputed element of the Christian awareness"; if "the existence of Satan and the demons has never been made the object of a dogmatic declaration", it was simply because it seemed superfluous, since the conviction was a common assumption, integral to "the constant and universal faith of the Church, which is based on its greatest source, namely, the teaching of Christ, and also on that concrete expression of lived faith, the liturgy, which has always insisted on the existence of demons and the threat which they represent."[5]

One year before his death Paul VI was to return to this topic in another general audience: "It is no wonder if our society is disintegrating when Holy Scripture sharply warns us that 'the whole world (in the pejorative sense) is under the power of the evil one' who is also called 'the prince of this world'."

Each time the reaction was one of uproar and protest: and strangely enough it came from precisely those newspapers and commentators which should have been unconcerned about the renewed emphasis on an aspect of a faith which

[3] Ibid.
[4] Ibid.
[5] Document of the Congregation for the Faith, June 1975.

they claimed to reject totally. From their point of view, irony would have been understandable; why the anger?

An ever-timely topic

It was the same this time, after we published our preview of Cardinal Ratzinger's position. He linked that sketch of his views with the discussion of a certain decline in missionary zeal, the result of what he called "an exaggerated shift of emphasis toward non-Christian religions" on the part of certain authors (the Prefect currently had Africa particularly in mind): "In any case we should beware of romanticizing the animist religions. Naturally they contain 'grains of truth', but in their concrete form they have created a world of fear, from which God is far removed and in which the earth is at the mercy of arbitrary spirits. Just as in the Mediterranean area in the time of the apostles, so in Africa the proclamation of Christ, who has conquered the 'spiritual powers' (Eph 6:12), was experienced as liberation from fear. The peace and innocence of paganism is one of the many myths of our day."

Ratzinger continued: "Whatever the less discerning theologians may say, the devil, as far as Christian belief is concerned, is a puzzling but real, personal and not merely symbolical presence. He is a powerful reality ('the prince of this world', as he is called by the New Testament, which continually reminds us of his existence), a baneful superhuman freedom directed against God's freedom. This is evident if we look realistically at history, with its abyss of evernew atrocities which cannot be explained by reference to man alone. On his own, man has not the power to oppose Satan, but the devil is not a second God, and united with Jesus we can be certain of vanquishing him. Christ is 'God who is

near to us', willing and able to liberate us: that is why the
Gospel really is 'Good News'. And that is why we must go
on proclaiming Christ in those realms of fear and unfreedom
which non-Christian religions often are. Furthermore, the
atheistic culture of the modern Western world is still surviving thanks to the liberation from the fear of demons which
Christianity brought about. If this redeeming light of Christianity were to fail, the world with all its knowledge and
technology would slip back into an inescapable fear in the
face of the alien impenetrability of being. There are already
signs of the return of these dark powers, and Satanic cults are
spreading more and more in the secularized world."

We are bound to inform our readers that statements of this
kind are completely in line with the Church's traditional
teaching, ratified by Vatican II, which speaks seventeen times
of "Satan", the "devil", the "evil one", the "ancient serpent",
the "power of darkness" and the "prince of this world". At
least five times these references occur in *Gaudium et spes*, the
most "optimistic" document of the entire Council.

As regards the non-Christian religions and the Christ
who is able to bring liberation from fear, it is quite correct
that Vatican II has happily ushered in a new phase of genuine dialogue with non-Christian religions. ("The Catholic
Church rejects nothing of what is true and holy in these
religions. She has a high regard for the manner of life and
conduct, the precepts and doctrines which, although differ-
ing in many ways from her own teaching, nevertheless often reflect a ray of that truth which enlightens all men"
Nostrae aetate, 2.) But in the Decree on Missionary Activity
(three times in the text and once in a footnote) the same
Council confirms the traditional teaching, which is also the
biblical teaching, as the Council illustrates it with numerous
scriptural texts: "God decided to enter into the history of

mankind in a new and definitive manner, by sending his
own Son in human flesh, so that through him he might
snatch men from the power of darkness and of Satan (cf. Col
1:13; Acts 10:38)." "Christ . . . who overthrows the rule of
the devil and limits the manifold malice of evil." We have
been "delivered from the powers of darkness through the
sacraments of Christian initiation . . ." (*Ad gentes,* 3,9 and
14). And with regard to our "having been delivered from
the powers of darkness", as the text puts it, an official footnote indicates five New Testament passages and the Roman
baptismal liturgy. We have said this out of a sense of duty to
provide objective information, though we are well aware
that it is always a risky matter (and can sometimes lead to
error) to cull quotations from their contexts.

As far as Ratzinger's reference to the present time is concerned ("Satanic cults are spreading more and more in the
secularized world"), anyone who is well informed knows
that, while the things that are coming to the surface and appear in the newspapers are disturbing enough, this is only
the tip of the iceberg, and its roots are in fact in the tech-
nologically most developed parts of the world, beginning in
California and Northern Europe.

All the detailed explanations we have given are necessary,
but at the same time they are fruitless if they are a priori
ignored by commentators who see any reference to these
disturbing realities as "medieval", whereby medieval is
naturally understood in the sense of the man in the street,
whose notion of the "Middle Ages" is still that suggested by
the pamphleteers and novelists of eighteenth- and nineteenth-
century Europe.

A suspicious "farewell"

Joseph Ratzinger, partly as a result of his extensive theological research, is not a man to be impressed by the reactions of journalists or of many an "expert". In a document signed by him we read the following exhortation taken from Holy Scripture: "Strong in faith, we must resist errors, even if they are presented in the guise of piety. Our only aim must be to do the truth in love and so to embrace those who err in the love of the Lord."

He by no means puts his observations on the devil at the center of his thought (well aware that what is decisive is the victory over him won by Christ), but a similar statement gives him the opportunity for an exemplary exposition of those theological methods which he regards as unacceptable. The "exemplary" nature of these remarks in our view justifies the space given to the topic. This issue, as we shall see, also involves eschatology, the indispensable Christian belief in the existence of a "beyond". This is no doubt why one of his most celebrated books, *Dogma und Verkündigung*, treats the traditional topic concerning the devil as one of the "major themes of preaching". It is for the same reason, surely, that, since becoming Prefect of the Congregation for the Faith, he has written the foreword to a book by his fellow Cardinal Léon Suenens concerned with affirming the Catholic doctrine of the devil as a "reality that is not symbolic but personal".

The Prefect told me about the famous little book in which a colleague of his, professor of exegesis at the University of Tübingen, intended to say, as he did in the title itself, "Farewell to the Devil". (He laughed heartily as he told me the following anecdote: among other things presented to him by his fellow professors at a small farewell party—on the occasion of his being appointed to the faculty of the

University of Regensburg — the above-mentioned book was presented to him by its author. The book's dedication read as follows: To my dear colleague Professor Joseph Ratzinger, to whom I find it harder to say farewell than to the devil. . . .)

Personal friendship with his colleague has not prevented him, then or now, from following his own line: "We must respect the experiences, sufferings, human decisions and also the practical necessities which lie behind certain theologies. But at the same time we must be utterly resolute in disputing that such theologies can still be called Catholic."

For him, the book written to bid farewell to the devil (which stands as one instance of a whole series that has reached the bookshops in recent years) is not "Catholic" because "the assertion which crowns the whole argument is superficial: 'We have already seen that the concept *devil* in the New Testament simply stands for the concept *sin*; the devil is only an image, a symbol, of this.' " Ratzinger reminds us that at that time, "when Paul VI was emphasizing the real existence of Satan and condemning the attempts to dissolve him into an abstract concept, it was the same theologian — expressing the views of many of his colleagues — who accused the Pope of slipping back into an archaic view of the world and confusing sin, which in Holy Scripture is part of the structure of faith, and Satan, which is only a historical, time-bound expression."

The Prefect remarks, however (referring to what he had already written as a theologian), that "if one carefully reads these books which are endeavoring to get rid of the disturbing diabolical presence, one ends up by being convinced of the opposite: the evangelists often speak in these terms and have not the least intention of speaking symbolically. Like Jesus himself they were convinced — and so they were determined to teach — that what was involved was a concrete power and certainly not an abstract concept. A power by which man is threatened and from which he is liberated by Christ, because he alone is the 'stronger man' who can bind the 'strong man', to use the words of the Gospel" (Lk 11:22).

"Exegetes or sociologists?"

If the teaching of Holy Scripture is as clear as this, how can one justify the replacement of the concrete term "Satan" by the abstract concept "sin"?

It is precisely here that Ratzinger discerns a methodology which is used by some contemporary exegesis and theology and which he rejects: "In this special case they admit—they have no choice—that Jesus, the apostles and the evangelists were convinced of the existence of demonic powers. Then they go on to take it for granted that in this conviction of theirs they were 'victims' of current Jewish ways of thinking. But since they have already taken it to be absolutely certain that 'this idea can no longer be reconciled with our view of the world', they have simply removed, by sleight of hand, whatever is regarded as unintelligible to today's average man."

Consequently, he goes on, "in 'saying farewell to the devil' they are not basing themselves on Holy Scripture (which supports just the opposite view) but on our world view. Thus they are saying farewell to every other aspect of faith which does not fit with the current conformism; and they do so, not as exegetes, as interpreters of Holy Scripture, but as contemporary men."

For Ratzinger, these methods lead to serious consequences: "Ultimately the authority on which these biblical scholars base their judgment is not the Bible itself but the *weltanschauung* they hold to be contemporary. They are therefore speaking as philosophers or sociologists, and their philosophy consists merely in a banal, uncritical assent to the convictions of the present time, which are always provisional."

If I have understood him correctly, this would be to stand the traditional method of theological study on its head: Scripture no longer judges the "world", but the "world" judges Scripture.

He comments: "They are constantly trying to find a message that represents what we already know, or at any rate what the listener wants to hear. As far as the devil is concerned, faith today, as always, holds fast to the mysterious but objective and disconcerting reality. But the Christian knows that the person who fears God needs fear nothing and no one. The fear of God is faith, something very different from a fear which enslaves, a fear of demons. But the fear of God is also very different from a pretentious daring which does not want to see the seriousness of reality. Genuine courage does not close its eyes to the dimensions of danger but considers danger realistically."

According to the Cardinal, the Church's pastoral practice must "find the appropriate language for a content that remains permanently valid: life is a serious business; we must be on our guard lest we reject the promise of eternal life offered to all, eternal friendship with Christ. We must not yield to the mentality of so many believers nowadays who think it is enough to act more or less like the majority and everything will automatically be all right."

He continues: "Catechesis must get back to being, not one opinion among others, but a certainty drawing on the Church's faith, the substance of which far surpasses accepted opinion. By contrast, modern catechesis to a large extent hardly mentions the concept of 'eternal life', and the problem of death is only touched upon, and then for the most part only in the context of how to delay its approach or mitigate its attendant conditions. Since many Christians have lost their sense for the 'last things', death is surrounded by silence, fear or the attempt to trivialize it. For centuries the Church has taught us to pray that death will not overtake us unawares, that we shall be given time to prepare for it; now, a sudden death is regarded as a blessing. If we do not accept and respect death, we do not accept and respect life either."

Purgatory and limbo

I have the impression, I tell the Cardinal, that Christian eschatology (insofar as it is mentioned at all) has been reduced to "heaven" alone, and even the word itself causes problems; it is written in quotation marks, and here too there are people who would reduce it to the level of an oriental myth. Obviously we would all be delighted if our future held no other possibility but eternal blessedness. In fact any one who reads the Gospels does find first and foremost *the* Good News, the consoling proclamation of the Father's infinite and immeasurable love. But side by side with it we also find in the Gospels the clear affirmation that disaster is possible and that it is not impossible to refuse God's love. Are not the Gospels, precisely because they are "true", both consoling and challenging writings, promises addressed to men who are free and therefore open to different destinies? Purgatory, for example; what has happened to Purgatory?

He shakes his head: "The fact is that all of us today think we are so good that we deserve nothing less than heaven! No doubt our civilization is responsible for this in that it focuses on mitigating circumstances and alibis in the attempt to take away people's sense of guilt, of sin. Someone remarked that today's dominant ideologies are constructed on a common fundamental dogma, namely, the stubborn denial of sin, i.e., that very reality with which belief in hell and Purgatory is associated. But the silence regarding Purgatory is also due to something else."

What is that?

"The *biblicism* which was first developed in the Protestant tradition and which has rapidly come into Catholic theology as well. Here people maintain that those explicit passages of Scripture about the state which tradition calls 'Purgatory' (the term is certainly a relatively late one, but the reality was evidently believed by Christians from the very beginning) are inadequate and insufficiently clear. But as I have said elsewhere, this *biblicism* has scarcely anything to do with the Catholic understanding, according to which the Bible must be read within the Church and her faith. My view is that if Purgatory did not exist, we should have to invent it."

Why?

"Because few things are as immediate, as human and as widespread—at all times and in all cultures—as prayer for one's own departed dear ones."

Calvin, the Reformer of Geneva, had a woman whipped because she was discovered praying at the grave of her son and hence was guilty, according to Calvin, of "superstition".

"In theory, the Reformation refuses to accept Purgatory, and consequently it also rejects prayer for the departed. In fact German Lutherans at least have returned to it in practice and have found considerable theological justification for it. Praying for one's departed loved ones is a far too immediate urge to be suppressed; it is a most beautiful manifestation of solidarity, love and assistance, reaching beyond the barrier of death. The happiness or unhappiness of a person dear to me, who has now crossed to the other shore, depends in part on whether I remember or forget him; he does not stop needing my love."

The concept of "indulgences", however, to be gained for oneself or on behalf of a deceased person, seems to have disappeared from religious practice and perhaps also from official catechesis.

"I would not say 'disappeared', but it has lost a lot of meaning since it is not plausible in terms of today's thinking. But catechesis has no right to surrender the concept. We need not be afraid to admit that—in a particular cultural context—pastoral practice has a hard time making a particular truth of faith understood. This may be the case with 'indulgences'. But the fact that there are problems translating a truth into current language in no way means that the truth concerned no longer exists. This applies to many other areas of faith."

Staying with eschatology for a moment: "limbo" has actually disappeared, that intermediate place where unbaptized children, i.e., those with only the "stain" of original sin, were supposed to go. For instance, we find no trace of it any longer in the official catechism of the Italian episcopate.

"Limbo was never a defined truth of faith. Personally—and here I am speaking more as a theologian and not as Prefect of the Congregation—I would abandon it since it was only a theological hypothesis. It formed part of a secondary thesis in support of a truth which is absolutely of first significance for faith, namely, the importance of baptism. To put it in the words of Jesus to Nicodemus: 'Truly, truly, I say to you, unless one is born of water and the Spirit, he cannot enter the Kingdom of God' (Jn 3:5). One should not hesitate to give up the idea of 'limbo' if need be (and it is

worth noting that the very theologians who proposed 'limbo'
also said that parents could spare the child limbo by desiring
its baptism and through prayer); but the concern behind it
must not be surrendered. Baptism has never been a side issue
for faith; it is not now, nor will it ever be."

A service for the world

Let us leave baptism and come back to sin and the uncomfortable subject we began with.

Rounding off his thoughts, Ratzinger says: "The more
one understands the holiness of God, the more one understands the opposite of what is holy, namely, the deceptive
masks of the devil. Jesus Christ himself is the greatest example of this: before him, the Holy One, Satan could not keep
hidden and was constantly compelled to show himself. So
one might say that the disappearance of the awareness of the
demonic indicates a related decline in holiness. The devil can
take refuge in his favorite element, anonymity, if he is not
exposed by the radiance of the person united to Christ."

Cardinal, I am really afraid that such expressions will only
lead to more and harsher accusations of "obscurantism".

"There is nothing I can do about that. I can only remind
you that such a 'detached' and 'modern' theologian as Harvey
Cox wrote—still in his secularizing, demythologizing phase—
that the 'mass-media (which are the reflection of our society),
by presenting particular models of conduct and recommending particular human ideals, are appealing to the unbanished
demons within and around us.' Cox himself says that, as a result, Christians 'need to return to clear words of exorcism'."

Dare I ask whether this means the rediscovery of exorcism as a kind of "social service"?

"Anyone who has a clear picture of the dark sides of the age in which we live sees forces at work which aim to disintegrate the relationships among men. In this situation the Christian can see that his task as exorcist must regain the importance it had when the faith was at its beginning. Of course the word 'exorcism' must not be understood here in its technical sense; it simply refers to the attitude of faith as a whole, which 'overcomes the world' and 'casts out' the prince of this world. Once the Christian has begun to be aware of this dark abyss, he knows that he owes the world this service. Let us not succumb to the popular idea that 'we can solve all problems with a little good will'. Even if we did not have faith, but were genuine realists, we would be convinced that, without the assistance of a higher power — which, for the Christian, is the Lord alone — we are prisoners of a baneful history."

Are you not inviting the charge of "pessimism"?

"By no means. If we remain united to Christ, we can be sure of victory. As Paul reiterates: 'Be strong in the Lord and in the strength of his might. Put on the whole armor of God, that you may be able to stand against the wiles of the devil' (Eph 6:10f.). If we look closely at the most recent secular culture, we see how the easy, naive optimism is turning into its opposite — radical pessimism and despairing nihilism. So it may be that the Christians who up to now were accused of being 'pessimists' must help their brothers to escape from this despair by putting before them the radical optimism which does not deceive — whose name is Jesus Christ."

Don't forget the angels

Someone once said that people always talk too much or too little about the devil. Having pilloried today's "too little", the Cardinal urges us to be aware of the opposite danger of "too much": "The mystery of evil must be seen in the total Christian context of the Resurrection of Jesus Christ and of his victory over the powers of evil. In this horizon the Christian's freedom, and his calm certainty 'which casts out fear' (1 Jn 4:18), can develop in all their dimensions: truth casts out fear and thus enables us to recognize the power of evil. If ambiguity is the mark of the demonic, the essence of the Christian's struggle against the devil lies in living day by day in the light of faith's clarity."

It has been pointed out that, lest Catholic truth become unbalanced, the faithful must be reminded of the other side of this truth, which the Church has always confessed in harmony with Holy Scripture, namely, the existence of God's good angels, spiritual beings living in fellowship with men, whose task is to assist them in their struggle.

Here, of course, we are in an area that modern sensibility, with the pretension of knowing everything, finds offensive. But in the realm of faith *tout se tient*: we cannot remove isolated stones from the whole edifice. As well as the angels who "fell" mysteriously, thus entering upon the dismal role of tempters, there is "the radiant sight of a spiritual army, joined in love to mankind". This realm occupies a broad area in the liturgy of the Christian West and East. To it belong the "guardian angels", objects of man's confident trust and a further proof of God's loving care for man. Each person has a guardian angel, and one of the most well-loved and widespread prayers of Christendom is addressed to this being. The consciousness of the People of God has always felt this beneficent presence to be a further and concrete sign of Providence, of the Father's concern for his children.

The Cardinal emphasizes, however, that "the reality opposed to the categories of the demonic is the third Person of the Trinity, the Holy Spirit." He explains: "Satan is the absolute destroyer, undermining every relationship: man's relationship to himself and men's relation to one another. Thus he is the exact opposite of the Holy Spirit, who is the absolute 'mediator' who guarantees the relationships in which all others are rooted and whence they spring: the trinitarian relationship by which Father and Son are One, one God in the unity of the Spirit."

The return of the Spirit

Nowadays, I notice, there is underway a rediscovery of the Holy Spirit, who has perhaps been rather forgotten in Western theology. This rediscovery has not been merely theoretical but has involved growing numbers of people in the so-called "Charismatic Movement" or "Renewal".

"That is so", he agrees. "The period following the Council scarcely seemed to live up to the hopes of John XXIII, who looked for a 'new Pentecost'. But his prayer did not go unheard. In the heart of a world dessicated by rationalistic scepticism a new experience of the Holy Spirit has come about, amounting to a worldwide renewal movement. What the New Testament describes, with reference to the charisms, as visible signs of the coming of the Spirit is no longer merely ancient, past history: this history is becoming a burning reality today."

"It is no accident", he stresses, in support of his view of the Spirit as the antithesis of the demonic, "that whereas a reductionist theology treats the devil and the world of evil spirits as a mere label, there is in the 'Renewal' a new and concrete awareness of the powers of evil, in addition, of course, to the calm certainty of the power of Christ who subjugates them all."

However, it is the Cardinal's official duty—here as elsewhere—to examine what may be the "other side of the coin". As far as the Charismatic Movement is concerned, "it is essential, above all, to maintain a balance, to beware of an exclusive emphasis on the Spirit, who, as Jesus himself reminds us, 'does not speak of himself' but lives and works at the heart of the life of the Trinity." A wrong overemphasis, he says, "could lead to setting against the hierarchically structured Church (which is based on Christ) a 'charismatic' Church based only on the 'freedom of the Spirit', a Church that regards herself as a continually new 'happening'."

"Maintaining balance also means keeping the proper relationship between institution and charism, between the Church's common faith and personal experience. Without personal experience doctrinal belief remains empty; pure experience is blind unless it is linked to the faith of the Church. What counts, ultimately, is not the 'we' of the group, but the great 'we' of the universal Church. She alone can provide the proper context in which we can 'not extinguish the Spirit and keep to what is good', as the apostle exhorts us."

Furthermore, he says, exploring the panorama of "risks", "We must beware of a too-easy ecumenism which can lead Catholic charismatic groups to lose their identity and, in the name of the 'Spirit' (seen as the antithesis of the institution), uncritically associate with forms of Pentecostalism of non-Catholic origin." Catholic renewal groups must therefore "think with the Church—*sentire cum ecclesia*—more than ever. They must always act in unity with the bishop, not least so that they will avoid the consequences that always arise when Holy Scripture is taken out of its context in the fellowship of the Church, which results in fundamentalism and the marks of the esoteric group and the sect."

Having given this warning about the risks involved, does the Cardinal also see positive signs in the emergence of the Charismatic Renewal Movement into the limelight of the Church's life?

"Certainly", he affirms. "It is evidence of hope, a positive sign of the times, a gift of God to our age. It is a rediscovery of the joy and wealth of prayer over against theories and practices which had become increasingly ossified and shriveled as a result of secularized rationalism. I myself have observed the effectiveness of the Movement: in Munich I saw a number of good vocations to the priesthood come from it. As I have already said, like every other reality entrusted to human beings, it too is exposed to misunderstandings, misinterpretations and exaggeration. But it would be dangerous to see only the risks and not also the gift offered by God. The necessary caution does not alter my fundamentally positive judgment."

CHAPTER ELEVEN

BRETHREN, BUT SEPARATED

A more "modern" Christianity?

Let us now turn to the ecumenical question, the relations between the various Christian confessions. As a citizen of a multi-denominational land like Germany, Joseph Ratzinger has already written a considerable amount on this subject. Today, in his new post, the ecumenical question is surely no less real.

"The ecumenical effort is an integral part of the development of faith in the present period of the Church's history." Here too, however, he feels the need for clarity, all the more so as the issues increase in importance. On one occasion he observed: "The further you proceed along the wrong path, the further you get from your destination." For himself, he is vigilant, he exercises his "critical function", convinced that—as everywhere else—"in the field of ecumenism, misunderstandings, impatience and arbitrary action are more likely to push the goal further away than to bring it nearer."

He is convinced that "clear definitions of one's own faith are of service to all, including one's partner in dialogue." Also that "dialogue can deepen and purify Catholic faith but cannot alter it in its true essence."

I begin with a provocative statement: "Your Eminence, there are people who say that a 'Protestantizing' process is at work in Catholicism." As usual, his answer goes to the heart of the question; he does not take refuge behind evasive "distinctions".

"The answer to this question depends on how you define the content of 'Protestantism'. Those who speak of a 'Protestantizing' of the Catholic Church nowadays probably see it as an alteration in the fundamental understanding of what is meant by 'Church', a different concept of the relationship between Church and Gospel. There is indeed a danger of this kind of alteration; it is not merely the caricature drawn by certain integralist circles."

But why should Protestantism—which is undergoing a crisis no less than the Catholic Church—attract theologians and believers who, up to the Council, had remained faithful to the Roman Church?

"It is not easy to say. The following consideration suggests itself to me: Protestantism arose at the beginning of modern times, and thus it is much more closely related to the inner energies which produced the modern age than Catholicism is. It has acquired the form it has today largely in the confrontation with the great philosophical currents of the nineteenth century. It is wide open to modern thought, and, as well as constituting a threat to it, that constitutes both its opportunity and its danger. So it is that those Catholic theologians, particularly, for whom their inherited theology no longer means anything, imagine that here they will find a path already blazed for the fusing of faith and modern thought."

What principles are involved here?

"Then as now the *sola scriptura* principle plays a key role. What today's average Christian deduces from this principle is that faith comes from one's individual perception, from intellectual application along with the contributions of experts, and a view such as this strikes him as more modern and more obvious than the Catholic position. Let us go deeper. Once this view has been adopted, the Catholic concept of the Church is automatically no longer tenable; a model of the Church must be sought elsewhere within the wide spectrum of the phenomenon of 'Protestantism'."

Ecclesiology then, as almost always, comes into the picture.

"Yes. For the modern man in the street, the most obvious concept of the Church is what technically one would call Congregationalist or Free Church. It implies that the Church is a changeable form depending upon how men organize what pertains to faith. Consequently one has to adapt as far as possible to the demands of the present moment. We have already mentioned this several times, but it is worthwhile returning to it: today many people can hardly understand any more that behind a human reality stands the mysterious divine reality. And as we know, this is the Catholic understanding of the Church, and it is far harder to accept than the one we have just outlined, which is not simply *the* Protestant understanding but one that has developed within the phenomenon of 'Protestantism'."

At the end of 1983—the 500th anniversary of the birth of Martin Luther—faced with the enthusiastic participation of many Catholics in the celebrations, not a few sharp tongues remarked that if the Reformer had been here today he could have taught the same things and had a university professorship as well. He could even have taught in a Catholic seminary. What does the Prefect say to this? Does he think that the Congregation over which he presides would have invited the Augustinian to an "informational conversation"?

He smiles. "Yes, I do think that even today we would have to speak with him very seriously, and that today too his teaching could not be regarded as 'Catholic theology'.

Otherwise there would be no need of the ecumenical dialogue, which is a way of getting into a critical discussion with Luther and asking how the great things in his theology can be held fast while what is un-Catholic can be overcome."

It would be interesting to know what aspects nowadays would lead the Congregation of the Faith to step in. He answers without hesitation: "At the risk of being wearisome, I think it would again be the question of ecclesiology. At the disputation in Leipzig, Luther's opponents demonstrated irrefutably that his 'new teaching' went not only against the papacy but also against tradition, expressed clearly by the Fathers and the Councils. Luther was compelled to admit this and then declared that even ecumenical councils had erred. This means that the authority of the exegete is put over the authority of the Church and her tradition."

Was that the moment in which the decisive split occurred?

"Yes, I believe it was the decisive moment. For it meant that the Catholic conviction that the Church is the authentic interpreter of Revelation's real meaning had been surrendered. Luther could no longer share that certainty which recognizes in the Church a community consciousness superior to private reflection and interpretation. Thus the relationship between the Church and the individual, between the Church and the Bible, is fundamentally altered. This is the point which the Congregation would have to pursue with Luther if he were alive, or rather, this is the point which, in the ecumenical conversations, we do discuss with him. This question is also naturally at the root of most of our conversations with Catholic theologians. Catholic theology interprets the Church's faith; where it departs from interpretation and becomes autonomous reconstruction, something entirely different is being done."

Some are reconsidering

Cardinal Ratzinger, allow me to continue to play the *agent provocateur*: some people say that in recent years ecumenism has often been a one-way street. On the Catholic side there have been apologies and pleas for forgiveness—and often enough with very good reason—whereas all we see on the Protestant side are renewed statements of its own position and a reluctance (so, at least, it seems) to take a new and critical look at the origins of the Reformation and the course it took.

"That may be true in part. A certain attitude in Catholic ecumenism after the Council was perhaps marked by a kind of masochism and a somewhat perverse need to declare itself guilty for all the catastrophes of past history. But with regard to the German situation, which I know from the inside, I must say that I enjoy friendship with truly spiritual Protestants, people whom I greatly respect. They have a really deep Christian life and also feel deeply the guilt all Christians share for the divisions which pain us. I am convinced, therefore, that it would be unjust to generalize the one-way street idea. On the Protestant side there is also a new receptivity toward elements that are fundamental to the Catholic faith."

What is the main subject of possible revision on the Protestant side?

"People are beginning to rediscover the necessity of a tradition, without which the Bible hangs in the air as one old book among many. This discovery is also helped forward by the fact that the Protestants are together with the Orthodox in the World Council of Churches in Geneva, an organization which comprises a large portion of the Christian Churches and communions. For 'Eastern Orthodoxy' is synonymous with 'tradition'."

"Furthermore", he goes on, "an exclusive insistence on the *sola scriptura* of classical Protestantism could not possibly survive, and today it is in crisis more than ever precisely as a result of that 'scientific' exegesis which arose in, and was pioneered by, the Reformed theology. This demonstrates how much the Gospels are a product of the early Church, indeed, how the whole of Scripture is nothing other than tradition. So much so that a number of Lutheran scholars seem to converge with the view of the Eastern Orthodox: not *sola scriptura* but *sola traditio*. There is also among Protestant theologians a rediscovery of authority, of something like a hierarchy (i.e., a sacramental spiritual office) and of the reality of the sacraments."

He smiles, as a thought strikes him: "When we Catholics said these things, it was hard for the Protestants to accept them. But when the Eastern Churches said them, they were listened to and studied with greater attention, possibly because people were not so suspicious of them. Thus their presence in the Geneva World Council shows itself to be providential."

So there is movement on the Protestant side too; are they moving toward positions which could one day be common to us all?

A realist in the good sense, Ratzinger is far from naive optimism: "Yes, there is movement, i.e., an admission of unfaithfulness to Christ on the part of all Christians, not only on the Catholic side. So far, however, the difference in the ways in which the Church is understood, as we have explained, has proved to be an insuperable barrier. It will always be hard, if not impossible, for a Reformed Christian to accept the priesthood as a sacrament and an indispensable precondition for the Eucharist.

"For to accept this he would have to accept the structure

of the Church founded on apostolic succession. For the present at least, the furthest progress achieved is the acceptance of a model of the Church based on apostolic succession seen as the better solution—but not as the only and indispensable one."

Once again, as a result of this currently more "acceptable" and more obvious view of the Church, Ratzinger considers that where Protestants and Catholics live side by side, the latter are more in danger of adopting the positions of the former. "Genuine Catholicism", he says, "is a highly sensitive balance, an attempt to unite aspects in life which seem to contradict one another and yet which guarantee the completeness of the Credo. Moreover, Catholicism calls for an attitude of faith which often conflicts radically with today's dominant view."

As an example he cites Rome's renewed refusal to allow "intercommunion", i.e., the possibility of a Catholic participating in the eucharist of a Reformed church. He says, "Even many Catholics regard this refusal as the final fruit of an intolerance that ought to belong to past history. Many people say to us, 'Don't be so harsh, so anachronistic!' But it is not a question of intolerance or of ecumenical reticence: the Catholic confession is that without the apostolic succession there is no genuine priesthood, and hence there can be no sacramental Eucharist in the proper sense. We believe that the Founder of Christianity himself wanted it this way."

A long road

We have already referred indirectly to the Eastern Orthodox Churches. What are relations like with them?

"Contacts with them are only superficially easier; in reality we are faced with grave problems. These Churches have an authentic doctrine, but it is static, petrified as it were. They remain faithful to the tradition of the first Christian millennium, but they reject later developments on the grounds that Catholics decided upon these developments without them. For them, questions of faith can only be decided by a 'really ecumenical' council, i.e., one which includes all Christians. Therefore they regard as invalid what Catholics have declared since the split. In practice they are in agreement with much of what has been defined, but they see it as restricted to the Churches dependent on Rome and not binding on them."

Here at least, surely, ecclesiology is not such an insuperable problem?

"Yes and no. True, they share with us the conviction of the necessity of the apostolic succession; they have a genuine episcopate and Eucharist. But they cling to the idea of *autocephaly*, according to which the Churches, even if they are united in faith, are also independent from one another. They cannot accept that the Bishop of Rome, the Pope, is the principle and center of unity in a universal Church understood as a *communio*."

Can we not expect, I ask, the beginnings of a reunion with the East in the foreseeable future?

"Humanly speaking I do not see how there could be complete union, beyond the initial phase of practical steps which have already been taken. This difficulty persists at the theological level; however, at the concrete level, in terms of actual living, the relations are easier, as we find where Catholics and Orthodox come into contact with each other (and perhaps even share the same persecution). While the different ecclesiologies remain separated on theological grounds, the Churches in practice maintain a lively exchange, since there is a reciprocal recognition of sacraments and intercommunion is possible (under certain conditions), by contrast with the situation with the communions which have resulted from the Reformation."

The Anglicans have always regarded themselves as the *bridge church* between the Protestant and the Catholic world; not long ago it seemed that reunion was only one step away.

"That is true. Now, however, at least one section of the Anglicans have seriously distanced themselves by introducing new norms concerning the remarriage of divorcees, women priests and other questions in the area of moral theology. Decisions have been made which have created a new gulf, and not only between Anglicans and Catholics but also between Anglicans and Orthodox, for the Orthodox almost always share the Catholic view in these matters."

After the Council, someone suggested that it would be sufficient, to rediscover unity with our separated brethren, for the Catholic Church to set out on the path of "reform". However, I have here a document on ecumenism from the Protestant point of view, recently published and approved by the Italian Waldensian and Methodist Churches. It says: "Although they claim to be based on the same Lord, Catholicism and Protestantism are two *different ways* of understanding and living Christianity. These different ways are not *complementary* but *alternative*."

What does Cardinal Ratzinger say to this?

"I say that it is unfortunately still the case. We must not mistake words for reality: theological progress and a few common documents do not signify a really thoroughgoing *rapprochement*. The Eucharist is life, and, so far, we cannot share this life with those who have such a different understanding of the Church and the sacraments. An ecumenism which does not face up to these difficulties, which men at present find insuperable, is full of dangers. Of course there were dangers in the situation prior to the Council, a situation characterized by isolation and rigidity, which left little room for fraternal relations."

But the Bible is Catholic

Some practical steps have been taken, such as the collaboration on common versions of the Bible by several denominations. What does Ratzinger think of these ecumenical editions?

"The only ecumenical version I have studied is the German one. It was primarily intended for liturgical use and for catechetics. In practice it seems to be used almost exclusively by Catholics; many Lutherans do not use it and prefer to stay with 'their' Bible."

Is this then another example of the ecumenical one-way street?

"The fact is that, here too, it is a mistake to have expectations that are too great. Holy Scripture lives in a community and needs a language. To a certain extent, every translation is also an interpretation. There are passages, as all scholars now agree, in which it is the translator speaking rather than the Bible. There are portions of Holy Scripture which demand a clear decision, an unequivocal stand; one cannot cover these things up or try to hide the difficulties under superficial solutions. People sometimes give the impression that the exegetes, with their historico-critical methods, have found the 'scientific' and hence the nonpartisan solution. This is not the case, however; every 'science' unavoidably depends upon a philosophy, an ideology. There is no neutrality, here least of all. Besides which, I can well understand why German Lutherans insist on their Luther Bible.

It is precisely its linguistic form which was the real unifying power behind Lutheranism down the centuries; to take it away would be to touch the very core of Lutheran identity. This translation has an entirely different status in its own community from what any translation can have among us. Furthermore, through the interpretation which it enshrines, it has to a certain extent limited even the effects of the *sola scriptura* principle and created a common understanding of the Bible, a common 'ecclesial' assimilation of it."

He adds, "We must have the courage to say once again that the Bible, taken as a whole, is 'Catholic'. If we accept it as it is, in the unity of all its parts, we are accepting the great Fathers of the Church and the way they read it. By doing this we are entering the Catholic world."

Dare I suggest that what you have just said will arouse suspicion in the minds of those who see it in terms of apologetics?

"No", he replies, "for it is not only my assertion, but one shared by not a few contemporary Protestant scholars, such as Heinrich Schlier for example, one of the favorite pupils of the Lutheran Rudolf Bultmann. By consistently applying the *sola scriptura* principle, Schlier discovered that 'Catholicism' was already present in the New Testament. For there, there is already the idea of a living Church to which the Lord has entrusted his living word. Certainly the idea that Holy Scripture is an archaeological fossil, a disparate collection of 'sources' to be researched from the point of view of archaeology and paleontology, is nowhere to be found in Holy Scripture! So it was out of inner consistency that Schlier entered the Catholic Church. Others of his Protestant colleagues did not go as far as this, but the presence of the phenomenon of Catholicism in the Bible is hardly disputed any more."

And you yourself, Cardinal Ratzinger, did you never feel attracted to Protestantism (as a boy, a young seminarian or even a theologian); did you never think of changing your Christian allegiance?

"Never!" he exclaims. "The Catholicism of my native Bavaria knew how to provide room for all that was human, both prayer and festivities, penance and joy. A joyful, colorful, human Christianity. Perhaps it was also because I am in no way a 'purist' and have breathed the Baroque atmosphere ever since I was a child. So, in spite of all my appreciation of Protestant friends, from the purely psychological point of view I have simply never been attracted to it. Not in theology either. While Protestantism certainly could give the impression of superiority and greater learning, I was more convinced by the great tradition of the Fathers and medieval masters."

Churches in disarray

In 1945 you were 18, i.e., you spent your childhood and youth in a Germany under the sway of nazism. What was your experience, as a Catholic, of that terrible milieu?

"I grew up in a family which really practiced its faith. The faith of my parents, of our Church, confirmed for me that Catholicism was a citadel of truth and righteousness against the realm of atheism and deceit which nazism represented. The collapse of the regime proved to me that the Church's premonitions were right."

But Hitler was from Catholic Austria, the Party was founded in Catholic Munich and flourished there. . . .

"All the same it would be very rash to regard it as a product of Catholicism. The poisonous seeds of nazism are not the fruit of Austrian and Southern German Catholicism but rather of the decadent cosmopolitan atmosphere of Vienna at the end of the monarchy. In this atmosphere Hitler looked with envy at the strength and resoluteness of the German North: Frederick II and Bismarck were his political idols. And it is well known that in the decisive elections in 1933 Hitler had no majorities in the Catholic states."

How do you explain that?

"First of all I am bound to say that the faithful core of the Lutheran Church played an outstanding part in resisting Hitler. I remember the Barmen Declaration of May 31, 1934, in which the 'Confessing Church' dissociated itself from the 'German Christians' and so performed a fundamental act of opposition to Hitler's totalitarian aspirations. On the other hand, the phenomenon of the 'German Christians' shows the particular threat to which Protestantism was exposed at the moment of the seizure of power. The idea of a national, i.e., Germanic, anti-Latin Christianity gave a handle to Hitler, as did the tradition of State churches and the very strong emphasis on obedience to authority which is part and parcel of the Lutheran tradition. From these aspects German Protestantism, and Lutheranism especially, was far more liable to succumb to Hitler's attack. A movement such as the 'German Christians' could never have arisen within the Catholic concept of the Church."

This does not alter the fact that the Protestants also distinguished themselves in opposing National Socialism.

"No one denies that. Precisely because it was as I have described, it required more personal courage for Protestants to resist Hitler. Karl Barth expressed this very clearly in his refusal to take the oath administered to State officials. This is why Protestantism in particular can point to great outstanding personalities in the ranks of those who resisted

Hitler. It also explains why, among average Christians, Catholics found it easier to stand firm in opposition to Hitler's doctrines. That era showed us something that history has continually confirmed: while the Catholic Church can make tactical pacts, for the sake of the lesser evil, even with repressive States, in the last analysis she reveals herself as a bastion against totalitarian derangement. By her very nature, in fact, she cannot become tied up with the State and must oppose a State which would compel her faithful to accept a single view. I myself have experienced this as a young Catholic in Nazi Germany."

CHAPTER TWELVE

A CERTAIN "LIBERATION"

An instruction to read

At the time our conversation with Cardinal Ratzinger took place in Brixen, the *Instruction Concerning Certain Aspects of Liberation Theology* had not yet been published—it was to be presented in September—although it was already complete and bears the date of August 6. As a result of a journalistic indiscretion, however, an article was published in which Ratzinger had given his personal views, as a theologian, on the problem. It had already been announced in the press that one of the most well-known exponents of this theology had been "invited to a colloquium".

Thus the topic of "liberation theology" had already taken up whole pages of newsprint, and after the presentation of the *Instruction* it was to arouse even more attention. And it is disappointing to note that many of the commentaries—even those from the most distinguished quarters—gave their opinion of the Congregation's document without ever having read it, or at best having read it in an incomplete and possibly partisan synopsis. Moreover, practically all the reports dealt only with the *political* implications of the document and ignored the *religious* reasons behind it.

Consequently the Congregation for the Faith decided to make no further commentary but to refer people to the text itself, which was as debated as it was misunderstood. The aim, therefore, was that the *Instruction* should be read; and we have been asked to urge the reader to read it, whatever his conclusions may be.

It seemed important to us, however, to make available a document which — though it became public through a "journalistic indiscretion", as we put it — has now become common property and is a faithful presentation of Joseph Ratzinger's thought (as a *theologian* and not as Prefect of the Congregation for the Faith), a text, moreover, that is not easy to find for the theological layman. It is a text that can help us to understand the Cardinal Prefect's personal thought in this significant area. Here more than ever the Prefect sees "the defense of orthodoxy as being really the defense of the poor, saving them pain and illusions which contain no realistic prospect even of material liberation."

Let us also point out what the *Instruction* says right at the beginning, in its foreword: "The Congregation for the Faith does not intend to give an exhaustive treatment of the wide subject of Christian freedom and liberation. It intends to do this in a later document, which will put all the wealth of teaching and practice in the proper light and in a *positive context*."[1]

So this is only the first part of a statement on this issue, remaining to be completed at a later date.

Futhermore, the "warning" which is contained in the first, "negative" part, "must in no way be interpreted as a condemnation of all those who, with high ideals and in the authentic spirit of the Gospel, desire to take up the preferential 'option for the poor'. It must not be used as a pretext by those who, in the face of the tragic and pressing problems of misery and injustice, hide behind an attitude of neutrality and indifference. On the contrary, it is motivated by the

---

[1] "Instruction of the Congregation for the Faith concerning Certain Aspects of Liberation Theology," preface.

certainty that the grave ideological aberrations which it is
denouncing will inevitably lead to a betrayal of the cause of
the poor. It is more than ever necessary that the innumer-
able Christians who are illuminated by their faith and are
determined to live a Christian life without reservations
should commit themselves to fight for justice, freedom and
human dignity out of love to their disinherited, oppressed
and persecuted brothers. More than ever, the Church intends to condemn the abuses, injustices and infringements
of freedom, wherever they occur and whoever instigates
them, and to fight with her distinctive means to defend and
promote human rights, particularly in the person of the
poor."[2]

The need of redemption

Before going on to present the "private" document of Ratzinger the theologian, let us see what clarity we have gained
from our conversation concerning the concept of "liberation". (Once more, our aim is to situate Ratzinger's position in a more general context.) The issue needs to be seen
in a worldwide spectrum, so that the specifically Latin
American problem, with its "liberation theologies", can be
more clearly defined.

" 'Liberation' ", says the Cardinal, "seems to be the
watchword taken up by all contemporary cultures on all
continents. Among the adherents of these cultures, the will
to seek 'liberation' penetrates theology in all the various
cultural areas of the world."

He goes on: "As I already mentioned in our conversation
on the crisis of morality, 'liberation' is also the key concept

[2] Ibid.

in the rich society of North America and Western Europe: liberation from religious ethics and hence from the limitations of man himself. But there is also a search for 'liberation' in Africa and Asia, where disengagement from Western traditions presents itself as a problem of liberation from the colonial inheritance at the same time as the search is going on for one's own identity. We shall speak more about this later. In South America, finally, 'liberation' is primarily understood in a social, economic and political sense. Thus the question of *soteriology*, that is, the problem of salvation, of redemption (or *liberation*, as they prefer to say), has become the central question of theology."

Whence, I ask, comes this narrow concentration upon one aspect? (Though it seems to be correct, for the very first words of the *Instruction* of August 6 say that "the Gospel of Jesus Christ is a message of freedom and a power of liberation".)[3]

"This happened, and is still happening", he answers, "because theology is attempting to reply to the most burning question of today's world, i.e., the problem that, in spite of all his efforts, man is in no way redeemed and is not free and experiences a growing alienation. We see this in all present forms of society. The fundamental experience of our epoch is precisely the experience of 'alienation', that is, the condition which Christianity expresses traditionally as the *lack of redemption*. It is the experience of a human existence that has cut itself loose from God, only to find, not freedom, but slavery."

These are hard words, I observe.

"And yet this is how things are if we view them realistically and do not try to hide the state of affairs. Anyway, Christians are particularly exhorted to be realistic. Taking

[3] Ibid.

note of the signs of the times also means rediscovering the courage to look reality in the face, to see what is positive and what is negative. And if we take this objective line, we shall see that the secularist liberation programs have one element in common: they are attempting to achieve this liberation exclusively in the immanent plane, in history, in this world. But it is precisely this limited view, restricted to history and lacking an opening to transcendence, that has brought man to his present state."

It remains a fact, I say, that this longing for liberation constitutes a challenge to be taken up; was not theology right to take it up and supply a Christian answer?

"Certainly, if the answer is really Christian. The need for salvation which is so widespread today expresses the authentic, albeit obscured, perception of the dignity of the human being, who is created as 'God's image and likeness', as the first book of Holy Scripture puts it. But the danger of some theologies is that they insist on the immanentist perspective, the exclusively earthly standpoint of secularist liberation programs. They do not and cannot see that from a Christian point of view, 'liberation' is above all and primarily liberation from that radical slavery which the 'world' does not notice, which it actually denies, namely, the radical slavery of sin."

The text of a "private theologian"

After this general assessment, let us return to liberation theology, that "phenomenon with an extraordinary number of layers", which, though attempting to spread throughout the whole of the Third World, has its "center of gravity in Latin America".

So we come back to that "private" document which preceded the *Instruction* of Fall 1984. We are reproducing it in full (in italics) in the following pages. It was originally intended for a strictly theological readership, which explains why the language is not always immediately intelligible to the layman. In our view, however, it is worthwhile for the nonspecialist to struggle through a few perhaps more complex passages. And we repeat: however the individual evaluates this document, it will help to situate the phenomenon of "liberation theology" in the vast panorama of world theology. Furthermore it clarifies the motives that lie behind the position adopted by the Congregation in a process that is already operating and envisages further "stages".

Preliminary Notes

1. *Liberation theology is a phenomenon with an extraordinary number of layers. There is a whole spectrum from radically marxist positions, on the one hand, to the efforts which are being made within the framework of a correct and ecclesial theology, on the other hand, a theology which stresses the responsibility which Christians necessarily bear for the poor and oppressed, such as we see in the documents of the Latin American Bishops' Conference (CELAM) from Medellín to Puebla. In what follows, the concept of liberation theology will be understood in a narrower sense: it will refer only to those theologies which, in one way or another, have embraced the marxist fundamental option. Here too there are many individual differences, which cannot be dealt with in a general discussion of this kind. All I can do is attempt to illuminate certain trends which, notwithstanding the different nuances they exhibit, are widespread and exert a certain influence even where liberation theology in this more restricted sense does not exist.*

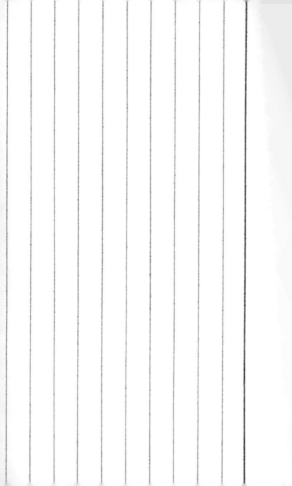

2. *An analysis of the phenomenon of liberation theology reveals that it constitutes a fundamental threat to the faith of the Church. At the same time it must be borne in mind that no error could persist unless it contained a grain of truth. Indeed, an error is all the more dangerous, the greater that grain of truth is, for then the temptation it exerts is all the greater.*

Furthermore, the error concerned would not have been able to wrench that piece of the truth to its own use if that truth had been adequately lived and witnessed to in its proper place (in the faith of the Church). So, in denouncing error and pointing to dangers in liberation theology, we must always be ready to ask what truth is latent in the error and how it can be given its rightful place, how it can be released from error's monopoly.

3. *Liberation theology is a universal phenomenon in three ways:*

a. It does not intend to add a new theological treatise to those already existing, i.e., it does not wish to develop new aspects of the Church's social ethics. Rather it sees itself as a new hermeneutics of the Christian faith, a new way of understanding Christianity as a whole and implementing it. Thus it affects theology in its basic constitution, not merely in aspects of its content. So too it alters all forms of Church life: the Church's constitution, liturgy, catechesis, moral options.

b. While liberation theology today has its center of gravity in Latin America, it is by no means an exclusively Latin American phenomenon. It is unthinkable apart from the governing influence of European and North American theologians. But it is also found in India, Sri Lanka, the Philippines, Taiwan and in Africa, though in the latter case the search for an "African theology" is in the foreground. The Union of Third World Theologians is strongly characterized by an emphasis on the themes of liberation theology.

c. Liberation theology goes beyond denominational borders:

from its own starting point it frequently tries to create a new universality for which the classical church divisions are supposed to have become irrelevant.

I. The concept of liberation theology and its origins and preconditions

These preliminary remarks have brought us right to the heart of the subject, without, however, dealing with the central question: what is liberation theology?

Initially we said that liberation theology intends to supply a new total interpretation of the Christian reality; it explains Christianity as a praxis of liberation and sees itself as the guide to this praxis. However, since in its view all reality is political, liberation is also a political concept and the guide to liberation must be a guide to political action:

"Nothing lies outside . . . political commitment. Everything has a political color." A theology that is not "practical", i.e., not essentially political, is regarded as "idealistic" and thus as lacking in reality, or else it is condemned as a vehicle for the oppressors' maintenance of power.

A theologian who has learned his theology in the classical tradition and has accepted its spiritual challenge will find it hard to realize that an attempt is being made, in all seriousness, to recast the whole Christian reality in the categories of politico-social liberation praxis. This is all the more difficult because many liberation theologians continue to use a great deal of the Church's classical ascetical and dogmatic language while changing its signification. As a result, the reader or listener who is operating from a different background can gain the impression that everything is the same as before, apart from the addition of a few somewhat unpalatable statements, which, given so much spirituality, can scarcely be all that dangerous.

The very radicality of liberation theology means that its seriousness is often underestimated, since it does not fit into any of the accepted categories of heresy; its fundamental concern cannot be detected by the existing range of standard questions.

I would like to try, therefore, to approach the basic orientation of liberation theology in two steps: first by saying something about its presuppositions, which make it possible, and then by referring to some of its basic concepts, which reveal something of its structure.

What could have led to that complete new orientation of theological thought that is expressed in liberation theology? In the main I see three factors which made it possible.

1. After the Council a new theological situation had arisen, again characterized by three assertions:

a. The view arose that the existing theological tradition was largely no longer adequate, and that, as a result, an entirely new theological and spiritual orientation needed to be sought directly from Scripture and from the signs of the times.

b. The idea of a turning to the world, of responsibility for the world, frequently deteriorated into a naive belief in science which accepted the human sciences as a new gospel without wanting to see their limitations and endemic problems. Psychology, sociology and the marxist interpretation of history seemed to be scientifically established and hence to become unquestionable arbiters of Christian thought.

c. The criticism of tradition applied by modern Evangelical exegesis, in particular by Rudolf Bultmann and his school, similarly became a firm theological authority, cutting off the path to theology in its prior form and so encouraging people all the more to produce new constructions.

2. *This changed theological situation coincided with a changed intellectual situation. At the end of the phase of reconstruction after the Second World War, which corresponded roughly to the end of the Council, a tangible vacuum of meaning had arisen in the Western world to which the still dominant existentialist philosophy could give no answer. In this situation the various brands of neo-marxism became a moral impulse, also holding out a promise of meaning that was practically irresistible to the academic youth. Bloch's marxism with its religious veneer and the strictly scientific appearance of the philosophies of Adorno, Horkheimer, Habermas and Marcuse offered models of action by which people believed they could respond to the moral challenge of misery in the world as well as realize the proper meaning of the biblical message.*

3. *The moral challenge of poverty and oppression presented itself in an ineluctable form at the very moment when Europe and North America had attained a hitherto unknown affluence. This challenge evidently called for new answers which were not to be found in the existing tradition. The changed theological and philosophical situation was a formal invitation to seek the answer in a Christianity which allowed itself to be guided by the models of hope — apparently scientifically grounded — put forward by marxist philosophies.*

II. The basic structure of liberation theology

This answer takes very different shapes, depending on the particular form of liberation theology, theology of revolution, political theology, etc. No overall description can be given, therefore. Yet there are certain basic concepts that recur in various modifications and express fundamental intentions held in common.

Before examining the content of these basic concepts we must make an observation concerning the cardinal structural elements of liberation theology, taking up what we have already said about the changed theological situation in the wake of the Council.

As I explained, the exegesis of Bultmann and his school now came to be read as the verdict of "science" on Jesus, a verdict that simply had to be accepted as valid. But Bultmann's "historical Jesus" is separated from the Christ of faith by a great gulf (Bultmann himself speaks of a "chasm"). In Bultmann, while Jesus is part of the presuppositions of the New Testament, he himself is enclosed in the world of Judaism.

Now the crucial result of this exegesis was to shatter the historical credibility of the Gospels: the Christ of the Church's tradition and the Jesus of history put forward by science evidently belong to two different worlds. Science, regarded as the final arbiter, had torn the figure of Jesus from its anchorage in tradition; on the one hand, consequently, tradition hangs in a vacuum, deprived of reality, while on the other hand, a new interpretation and significance must be sought for the figure of Jesus.

Bultmann's importance, therefore, was less because of his positive discoveries than because of the negative result of his criticism: the core of faith, christology, was open to new interpretations because its previous affirmations had perished as being historically no longer tenable. It also meant that the Church's teaching office was discredited, since she had evidently clung to a scientifically untenable theory, and thus ceased to be regarded as an authority where knowledge of Jesus was concerned. In the future her statements could only be seen as futile attempts to defend a position which was scientifically obsolete.

Another key word made Bultmann important for future developments. He had reinstated the old concept "hermeneutics" and given it a new thrust. The word hermeneutics expresses the insight that a real understanding of historical texts does not come about by mere historical interpretation and, indeed, that

*every historical interpretation already includes certain prior deci-
sions. Once the historical material has been established, it is the
task of hermeneutics to "actualize" Scripture. In classical ter-
minology, it is to "dissolve the horizon" between then and now.
It asks the question: what significance have these past events for
today? Bultmann himself had answered this question with the
help of Heidegger's philosophy and had interpreted the Bible in
a correspondingly existentialist manner. This answer attracted no
interest then, nor does it now; to that extent Bultmann has been
superseded in the exegesis currently acceptable. Yet what has remained is the abstraction of the figure of Jesus from the classical
tradition as well as the idea that, using a new hermeneutics, we
can and must bring this figure into the present in a new way.*

*At this point we come to the second element of our situation
to which we have already referred: the new philosophical climate
of the late sixties. In the meantime the marxist analysis of
history and society was largely accepted as the only "scientific"
one. This means that the world must be interpreted in terms of
the class struggle and that the only choice is between capitalism
and marxism. It also means that all reality is political and has to
justify itself politically. The biblical concept of the "poor" pro-
vides a starting point for fusing the Bible's view of history with
marxist dialectic; it is interpreted by the idea of the proletariat in
the marxist sense and thus justifies marxism as the legitimate
hermeneutics for understanding the Bible.*

*Since, according to this view, there are, and can only be, two
options, any objection to this interpretation of the Bible is an expression of the ruling class's determination to hold on to its
power. A well-known liberation theologian asserts: "The class
struggle is a fact; neutrality on this point is simply impossible."*

*This approach also takes the ground from under the feet of
the Church's teaching office: if she were to intervene and proceed
against such an interpretation of Christianity, she would only*

prove that she is on the side of the rich and the rulers and against the poor and suffering, i.e., against Jesus himself: she would show that she had taken the negative side in the dialectic of history.

This decision, apparently unavoidable in "scientific" and "historical" terms, automatically determines how Christianity shall be interpreted in the future, as regards both the activities of this interpretation and its content.

As far as the arbiters are concerned, the crucial concepts are people, community, experience and history. Previously it was the Church, namely, the Catholic Church in her totality — a totality which spanned time and space and embraced laity (sensus fidei) and hierarchy (Magisterium) — that constituted the hermeneutical criterion; now it is the "community". The experience of the "community" determines the understanding and the interpretation of Scripture.

Again it can be said, in a way that seems strictly scientific, that the Gospels' picture of Jesus is itself a synthesis of event and interpretation, based on the experience of the individual communities, whereby interpretation was far more important than the no longer ascertainable event.

This original synthesis of event and interpretation can be dissolved and reformed continually: the community "interprets" the events on the basis of its "experience" and thus discovers what its "praxis" should be. The same idea appears in a somewhat modified form in connection with the concept of the "people", where the conciliar emphasis on the "People of God" is transformed into a marxist myth. The experiences of the "people" elucidate Scripture. Here "people" is the antithesis of the hierarchy, the antithesis of all institutions, which are seen as oppressive powers. Ultimately anyone who participates in the class struggle is a member of the "people"; the "Church of the people" becomes the antagonist of the hierarchical Church.

Finally the concept "history" becomes a crucial interpretative category. *The view, accepted as scientifically certain and incontrovertible, that the Bible speaks exclusively in terms of salvation history (and thus, antimetaphysically), facilitates the fusing of the biblical horizon with the marxist idea of history, which progresses in a dialectical manner and is the real bringer of salvation. History is accordingly a process of progressive liberation; history is the real revelation and hence the real interpreter of the Bible. Sometimes this dialectic of progress is supported by pneumatology. In any case the latter also makes a teaching office which insists on abiding truths into an authority inimical to progress, thinking "metaphysically" and hence contradicting "history". We can say that the concept of history swallows up the concepts of God and of Revelation. The "historicality" of the Bible must justify its absolute dominance and thus legitimize the transition to materialist-marxist philosophy, in which history has taken over the role of God.*

III. Central concepts of liberation theology

So we have arrived at the basic concepts of the new interpretation of the Christian reality. Since the individual concepts occur in different contexts, I will simply discuss them one after another, without any systematization. Let us begin with the new meaning of faith, hope and love. Concerning faith, *one South American theologian says, for instance, that Jesus' experience of God is radically historical. "His faith is transformed into fidelity." Thus faith is fundamentally replaced by "fidelity to history". Here we see that fusion between God and history which makes it possible to keep the Chalcedonian formula for Jesus, albeit with a totally changed meaning: it is clear that the classical tests for orthodoxy are of no avail in analyzing this theology. It is asserted "that Jesus is God, but it is immediately added that the true and only God is he who reveals himself historically and as a stumbling block in Jesus, and in the poor who prolong his presence. Only the person who holds together these two affirmations is orthodox."*

Hope *is interpreted as "confidence in the future" and as working for the future and thus is subordinated once more to the history of class conflict.*

Love *consists in the "option for the poor", i.e., it coincides with opting for the class struggle. In opposition to "false universalism", the liberation theologians emphasize very strongly the partiality and partisan nature of the Christian option; in their view, taking sides is the fundamental presupposition for a correct hermeneutics of the biblical testimony. Here, I think, one can see very clearly that amalgam of a basic truth of Christianity and an un-Christian fundamental option which makes the whole thing so seductive: The Sermon on the Mount is indeed God taking sides with the poor. But to interpret the "poor" in the sense of the marxist dialectic of history, and "taking sides with them" in the sense of the class struggle, is a wanton attempt to portray as identical things that are contrary.*

The fundamental concept of the preaching of Jesus is the *"Kingdom of God". This concept is also at the center of the liberation theologies, but read against the background of marxist hermeneutics. According to one of these theologians, the Kingdom must not be understood in a spiritualist or universalist manner, not in the sense of an abstract eschatological eventuality. It must be understood in partisan terms and with a view to praxis. The meaning of the Kingdom can only be defined by reference to the praxis of Jesus, not theoretically: it means working at the historical reality that surrounds us in order to transform it into the Kingdom.*

Here we must mention another basic idea of a particular post-*conciliar theology which has led in this direction. People said that after the Council every* dualism *must be overcome: the dualism of body and soul, of natural and supernatural, of this world and the world beyond, of then and now. Once these supposed dualisms had been eliminated, it only remained to work for a kingdom to be realized in present history and in politico-economic reality. This meant, however, that one had ceased to work for the benefit of people in this present time and had begun to destroy the present in the interests of a supposed future: thus the real dualism had broken loose.*

In this connection I would like to mention the interpretation of death and resurrection given by one of the leading liberation theologians. First of all he once again opposes "universalist" conceptions by asserting that resurrection is in the first place a hope for those who are crucified, who make up the majority of men: all the millions who are subjected to a slow crucifixion by structural injustice. But faith also participates in Jesus' lordship over history by setting up the Kingdom, that is, by fighting for justice and integral liberation, by transforming unjust structures into more human ones. This lordship over history is exercised by repeating in history the gesture by which God raised Jesus, i.e., by giving life to those who are crucified in history. Man has taken over God's gesture — this manifests the whole transformation of the biblical message in an almost tragic way, when one thinks how this attempted imitation of God has worked out in practice and continues to do so.

As to other reinterpretations of biblical concepts: The Exodus *becomes the central image of salvation history; the* paschal mystery *is understood as a revolutionary symbol, and consequently the* Eucharist *is interpreted as a celebration of liberation in the sense of politico-messianic hope and praxis. The word* redemption *is largely replaced by* liberation, *which is seen, against the background of history and the class struggle, as a process of progressive liberation. Absolutely fundamental, finally, is the stress on* praxis: *truth must not be understood metaphysically, for that would be "idealism". Truth is realized in history and its praxis.* Action is truth. *Hence even the ideas which are employed in such action are ultimately interchangeable. Praxis is the sole deciding factor. The only true* orthodoxy *is therefore* orthopraxy. *It follows that the biblical texts can be treated more loosely, for historical criticism has loosed Scripture from the traditional interpretation, which now appears to be unscientific. Tradition itself is treated with the greatest possible scientific strictness along the lines of Bultmann. But as for the historically transmitted content of the Bible, it cannot be exclusively binding. Ultimately, what is normative for interpretation is not historical research but the hermeneutic of history experienced in the community or the political group.*

In trying to arrive at an overall evaluation it must be said that, if one accepts the fundamental assumptions which underlie liberation theology, it cannot be denied that the whole edifice has an almost irresistible logic. By adopting the position of biblical criticism and of a hermeneutics that grows through experience, on the one hand, and of the marxist analysis of history, on the other, liberation theologians have succeeded in creating a total picture of the Christian reality, and this total view seems to respond fully both to the claims of science and to the moral challenges of our time, urging people to make Christianity an instrument of concrete world transformation; it seems to have united Christianity, in this way, with all the "progressive forces" of our era. One can understand, therefore, that this new interpretation of Christianity should have exercised an increasing fascination over theologians, priests and religious, particularly against the background of Third World problems. To say "no" to it must seem to them to be a flight from reality as well as a denial of reason and morality. On the other hand, if one considers how radical this reinterpretation of Christianity is, it is all the more pressing to find the right answer to the challenge which it presents. We shall only survive this crisis if we succeed in making the logic of faith visible in an equally compelling manner and in presenting it as a logic of reality, i.e., manifesting the concrete force of a better answer attested in lived experience. Since it is so, since thought and experience, interpretation and realization, are equally called for, it is a task for the whole Church. Theology alone is insufficient, Church authority alone is insufficient. Since the phenomenon of liberation theology indicates a lack of conversion in the Church, a lack of radical faith, only an increase in conversion and faith can arouse and elicit those theological insights and those decisions on the part of the shepherds which will give an answer to the magnitude of the question.

Between marxism and capitalism

This, then, is the framework of reflections and observations forming the background to the now celebrated *Instruction Concerning Certain Aspects of Liberation Theology*.

It is important to add that, during our conversation with the Cardinal, a point often came up that has been forgotten by many commentators: "In those forms of it which are dependent on marxism, liberation theology is by no means a native, home-grown product of Latin America or of other underdeveloped areas; it is not something that has come from the people and grown spontaneously. Originally at least it was the creation of intellectuals, and intellectuals who were born or educated in the rich West. The theologians who started it are Europeans; the theologians who are promoting it in South America are Europeans or have been educated in European universities. Behind the Spanish or Portuguese language of their preaching one senses German, French and Anglo-American ideas."

For Ratzinger, therefore, liberation theology too is part of that "export to the Third World of myths and utopias which have been worked out in the developed West. It is as it were an attempt to test, in a concrete scenario, ideologies that have been invented in the laboratory by European theoreticians. In a certain respect, therefore, it is a kind of cultural imperialism, even if it is portrayed as the spontaneous creation of the disenfranchised masses. It would be important to examine what real influence is in fact exercised over the people by those theologians who maintain that they represent them as their spokesmen."

He continues in this vein with the observation that, "in the West, the marxist myth has lost its attraction for the young and even for the workers. There is an attempt, therefore, to export it to the Third World on the part of those intellectuals who actually live outside countries dominated by 'real Socialism'. Indeed, it is only where marxism-leninism is *not* in control that there are still people who take its illusory 'scientific truths' seriously."

He points out that "it is a paradox—albeit not too much of one—that faith seems to be more secure in the East, where it is officially persecuted. At the doctrinal level there are practically no problems with Catholicism in those regions. There is no danger that Christians there will go over to the principles of a culture achieved by coercion; there, every day, people pay the price, in their own flesh, for the tragedy of a society which has attempted a liberation, but a liberation from God. Indeed, the idea of a 'liberation theology' seems to be springing up in certain countries of the Eastern bloc, but there it is liberation from marxism. And it certainly does not mean that they are sympathetic toward the dominant ideologies and life patterns of the West."

He reminds me that "the Primate of Poland, Cardinal

Stefan Wyszynski, warned of the dangers of Western hedon-
ism and permissiveness no less than of marxist oppression.
Alfred Cardinal Bengsch of Berlin once said to me that he
saw a greater danger in Western consumerism and a theology infected by it than in marxist ideology."

Ratzinger is not afraid, either, to see "a sign of the
Satanic in the way in which people exploit the market for
pornography and drugs in the West". "There is something
diabolical in the coldblooded perversity with which man is
corrupted for the sake of money and profit is drawn from
his weakness, his temptability and vulnerability in the face
of temptation. Western culture is hellish when it persuades
men that the sole aim of life is pleasure and self-interest."

But if one asks him which of the many atheisms of our
time—at the theoretical level—seems the most deadly to
him, he comes back to marxism: "It seems to me that, in its
philosophy and its moral goals, marxism represents a more
insidious temptation than many practical atheisms which
are consequently less ambitious intellectually. For the marxist ideology actually uses the Jewish-Christian tradition and
turns it into a godless prophetic movement; man's religious
energies are used as a tool for political ends and directed to a
merely earthly hope, which is equivalent to standing on its
head the Christian yearning for eternal life. This perversion
of the biblical tradition deludes many believers who are convinced in good faith that the cause of Christ is the same as
that proclaimed by the heralds of political revolution."

An impossible dialogue

At this point—and with a depressed, rather than an "inquisi-
torial", mien—he once again reminded me of the "drama"

involved in the exercise of the Magisterium, illustrated by the following events: "It is always painfully difficult to enter into a conversation with those theologians who cling to that illusory myth which blocks the path of the reforms and intensifies misery and injustices, namely, the myth of the class struggle as an instrument in creating a classless society." He continues: "When one tries in a fraternal manner to indicate these aberrations by reference to the Bible and tradition, one is quickly labeled a 'servant', a 'lackey' of the ruling classes who, in order to secure their power, maintain the support of the Church. Most recent experience shows, however, that important representatives of liberation theology, because of their desire to be part of the Church's fellowship and to be of genuine service to man, dissociate themselves, happily, from the intransigence of a part of the mass-media and countless groups of predominantly European party followers. As to the latter, however carefully and respectfully we put our point of view, they always reject it a priori, lest they should seem to be going over to the side of the 'masters'. Thus the cause of the lowliest is betrayed by the very ideologies which have always proved to be the source of the people's suffering."

He then went on to tell me how dismayed he was by reading many of these theologians: "A continual refrain is this: 'Man must be liberated from the chains of politico-economic oppression; the reforms are not enough to liberate him, indeed they lead away from liberation; what is necessary is revolution, and the only way to bring about a revolution is to summon people to the class struggle.' Yet those who repeat all this seem to have no concrete and practical idea how a society could be organized after the revolution. They limit themselves to repeating that the revolution must be brought about."

Again he says: "What is theologically unacceptable here, and socially dangerous, is this mixture of Bible, christology, politics, sociology and economics. Holy Scripture and theology cannot be misused to absolutize and sacralize a theory concerning the socio-political order. Of its very nature, that order is always contingent. By sacralizing the revolution—mixing up God, Christ and ideologies—they only succeed in producing a dreamy fanaticism that can lead to even worse injustices and oppression, ruining in the praxis what the theory had proposed."

He goes on: "It is also painful to be confronted with the illusion, so essentially un-Christian, which is present among priests and theologians, that a new man and a new world can be created, not by calling each individual to conversion, but only by changing the social and economic structures. For it is precisely personal sin that is in reality at the root of unjust social structures. Those who really desire a more human society need to begin with the root, not with the trunk and branches, of the tree of injustice. The issue here is one of fundamental Christian truths, yet they are deprecatingly dismissed as 'alienating' and 'spiritualistic'."

CHAPTER THIRTEEN

PROCLAIMING CHRIST AGAIN

In defense of the missions

The South American liberation theology has also spread to parts of Asia and Africa. But here, as Ratzinger has already pointed out, "liberation" is understood primarily as a turning away from the European colonial inheritance. "People are passionately seeking for a proper 'inculturation' of Christianity. Hence we are faced with a new aspect of the old problem of the relationship between faith and history, faith and culture."

Outlining the problem, he remarks: "It is well enough known that the Catholic faith, as we know it today, developed chiefly from a Jewish root and then under the influence of the Graeco-Latin civilization; from the eighth century onward Irish and Germanic elements played their part in its formation to a not insignificant degree. Thus Africa (which only began really to be evangelized in the last two centuries) received a Christianity that had developed for 1800 years in a civilization alien to it. This Christianity was imparted to it in even the smallest detail. Moreover the faith arrived in Africa in the context of a colonial past which is now seen above all as a history of alienation and oppression."

And isn't that true, I ask?

"Not directly, as far as the Church's missionary activity is concerned", he replies. "With regard to the relationship between missionary activity and colonialism, false historical judgments are current right up to the present day, above all in Europe and America—less in Africa itself. Colonialism's abuses were actually moderated by the fearless activity of so many apostles of faith. They were often able to create oases of humanity in areas which had been ruined by the older misery and the newer oppression. One cannot simply forget, let alone condemn, the shining sacrifice of countless missionaries who became real fathers to the people entrusted to them. I continually meet Africans, both young and old, who tell me with great enthusiasm of those 'fathers' of their people who no doubt were tremendously human as well as heroic missionary figures. Among those whom they evangelized and tried to help in every way, often at the cost of their own lives, their memory is not extinguished. And if a certain friendship is still possible between Africa and Europe, it is due in part to those instances of self-sacrifice, which for the most part are known to God alone."

All the same it is a fact that it was Western Catholicism that was exported to those regions.

"We are well aware of this problem today", he says. "But what else could the missionaries of those times have done but to begin with the only catechism they knew? Nor should we forget that all of us have received the faith 'from outside': it comes to us from its Semitic homeland, from Palestine, mediated by Hellenism. The Nazis knew this only too well and tried to obliterate Christianity in Europe precisely because of its 'foreign' character."

A Gospel for Africa

He is aware, however, that "many people today in the Third World, and above all in Africa, are urgently asking:

'How can Christianity become an expression of our own faith? How can it fully and completely enter into our own identity? How binding is the cultural expression it has exhibited hitherto? To what extent can we, in a sense, speak of beginning our Christian history again? And could not *our* Old Testament be not so much the history of the Jewish people as the suffering history of our people and its traditional forms?' "

How, then, does the Cardinal evaluate the answers which Africans are giving to these questions as time goes by?

He says: "The problems are quite clear, but it must be said that the desired *théologie africaine,* or *African theology,* is at present more a project than a reality. Furthermore, if we look more closely, we must say that very much of what is regarded as 'African' is really a European import and has far less to do with actual African traditions than the classical Christian tradition has. The latter is de facto much nearer to the basic concepts of all mankind, much nearer to the fundamental inheritance of human religious culture in general, than the late constructions of European thought, which are often cut off from mankind's spiritual roots."

If I understand you correctly, you are making a defense of the "universal" significance of Christian thought as it has evolved in the West.

"We must recognize that there is no way back to the cultural situation which existed before the results of European thought spread to the whole world, as has been the case now for some time. On the other hand it must also be recognized that there is no such thing as 'pure' African tradition as such: it is a many-layered reality and consequently — depending on the particular layer and origin — it is often contradictory."

"There are two questions. First there is the question of

what is originally African, and hence what must be defended against the false claim to universality on the part of what is simply European. Conversely there is the question of what, although it is European, is actually universal. These questions are subject not only to human evaluation but also — as always — to the criterion of faith, which judges all traditions, all inheritances, ours and others'. As well as that, we must beware of over-hasty decisions and conclusions, for the problem is not only a matter of theory: its solution also requires the living, suffering and loving of the whole fellowship of believers, in the sense of the great Catholic principle which has been forgotten nowadays, namely, that theology's subject is not the individual theologians but the totality of the whole Church."

It is well known that the Congregation is somewhat uneasy about the formation of an ecumenical Association of African Theologians which unites African scholars of all denominations.

"The Association of Theologians to which you refer", he says, "does indeed raise many questions. As with other initiatives in other parts of the world, there is the danger that the search for an 'ecumenical' fellowship may cause the value of the great Catholic unity to be neglected in favor of limited cultural and national communities. With an Association of this kind we cannot exclude the possibility that the common awareness of what is regarded as 'African' may put the common awareness of what is Catholic in the shade. And all this is in spite of the fact, I repeat, that Africa is such a many-layered continent that it cannot be squeezed into a single overall framework."

From various quarters — and also, for some time, on the part of some African bishops — it has been proposed to summon a great African council.

"Yes, but so far the idea has no definite outlines. Initially it was promoted by the Association of Theologians we mentioned, and since then it has also found increasing support among a few bishops (though with corresponding modifications and more precision in matters of detail). In the Conferences of Medellín and Puebla, Latin America has shown that the work of the bishops of a continent can make a substantial contribution toward clarifying fundamental problems and properly fulfilling the pastoral task. So it seems quite possible — on the basis of experience gained in other regions — to provide a juridical and theological form for the idea of an African council (or, more precisely, an African *synod*), thus lending it full significance."

What are the central issues to be attended to, given the vast and vibrant area of Africa?

"The main areas are moral theology, liturgy and sacramental theology. Thus there is discussion of ways of transition from traditional polygamy to Christian monogamy, as well as questions regarding the form whereby marriage is concluded, and the adoption of African traditions in liturgy and popular spirituality."

Let us begin with polygamy. What are the issues here?

"It is clear that the conversion of polygamists to Christianity creates difficult legal and human problems. It is important here not to confuse polygamy with sexual license in the sense of the Western world. It is a socially and legally regulated institution, determining the relationship between husband, wife and children. But from the point of view of Christian faith it is an inadequate moral form which does not do justice to the husband-wife relationship. Recently some theologians (chiefly Europeans) have developed the idea that polygamy can also be a Christian form of marriage and family. But the African bishops and a majority of the theologians see quite clearly that this would not be a positive 'Africanization' of Christianity but a fixation at a stage of social development which has been overcome by the Gospel. Whereas here the discussion is being carried on with (aggressive enough) fringe groups, there is a far more serious problem in the connection between the sacramental form of Christian marriage and the tribal customs regarding marriage. There was already a wide discussion of this issue at the 1980 Synod of Bishops, and the search for appropriate solutions must go on. Then more and more significance attaches to the debate as to whether the worship of ancestors can be taken into the Christian faith-structure in any form. The veneration of saints and prayer for the departed souls create bridges here which make a fruitful exchange of ideas possible. Then again there are discussions as to how far and in what way elements of local tradition, apart from the case of marriage, can enter into the other sacraments."

"There is but one Savior"

We have spoken about the missionaries of the past and — with all its problems — the Catholicism of the present. In these years following the Council, however, the discussion seems to be dominated by the question of the Church's motives in her practical response to non-Christians. It is surely no secret that missionaries are suffering from a very tangible identity crisis and even a lack of motivation. . . .

His answer manifests a considerable concern: "It is part of the Church's ancient, traditional teaching that every man is called to salvation and de facto can be saved if he sincerely follows the precepts of his own conscience, even without being a visible member of the Catholic Church. This teaching however, which (I repeat) was already accepted and beyond dispute, has been put forward in an extreme form since the Council on the basis of theories like that of 'anonymous Christians'. Ultimately it has been proposed that grace is always given provided that a person believing in no religion at all or subscribing to any religion whatsoever — accepts himself as a human being. That is all that is necessary. According to these theories the Christian's 'plus' is only that he is *aware* of this grace, which inheres actually in all people, whether baptized or not. Hand in hand, then, with the weakening of the necessity of baptism, went the overemphasis on the values of the non-Christian religions, which many theologians saw not as *extraordinary* paths of salvation but precisely as *ordinary* ones."

With what results?

"Naturally, hypotheses of this kind caused the missionary zeal of many to slacken. Many a one began to wonder, 'Why should we disturb non-Christians, urging them to accept baptism and faith in Christ, if their religion is *their* way to salvation in their culture, in their part of the world?' Thus people surrendered, among other things, the connection which the New Testament creates between *salvation* and *truth*, for as Jesus explicitly affirms, it is knowledge of the truth that liberates and hence saves. Or as St. Paul says: 'God Our Savior . . . desires all men to be saved and to come to the knowledge of the truth.' And this truth, the Apostle goes on, consists in the knowledge that 'there is one God, and there is one mediator between God and men, the man Christ Jesus, who gave himself as a ransom for all' (1 Tim 2:4–7). This is what we must proclaim to the modern world, with humility but also with power, in response to the challenging example of the generations who have gone before us in faith."